Doñana

Doñana

SPAIN'S WILDLIFE WILDERNESS

Juan Antonio Fernández

with a foreword by Sir Peter Scott

Collins   St. James's Place, London   1975

Doñana, located where two continents meet, is at the confluence of the Afro-European migratory routes.

Copyright ©1974 Editorial Olivo - Sevilla
English translation copyright ©1975 Editorial Olivo - Sevilla
All rights reserved. Printed in Spain
ISBN 0 00 216117 6

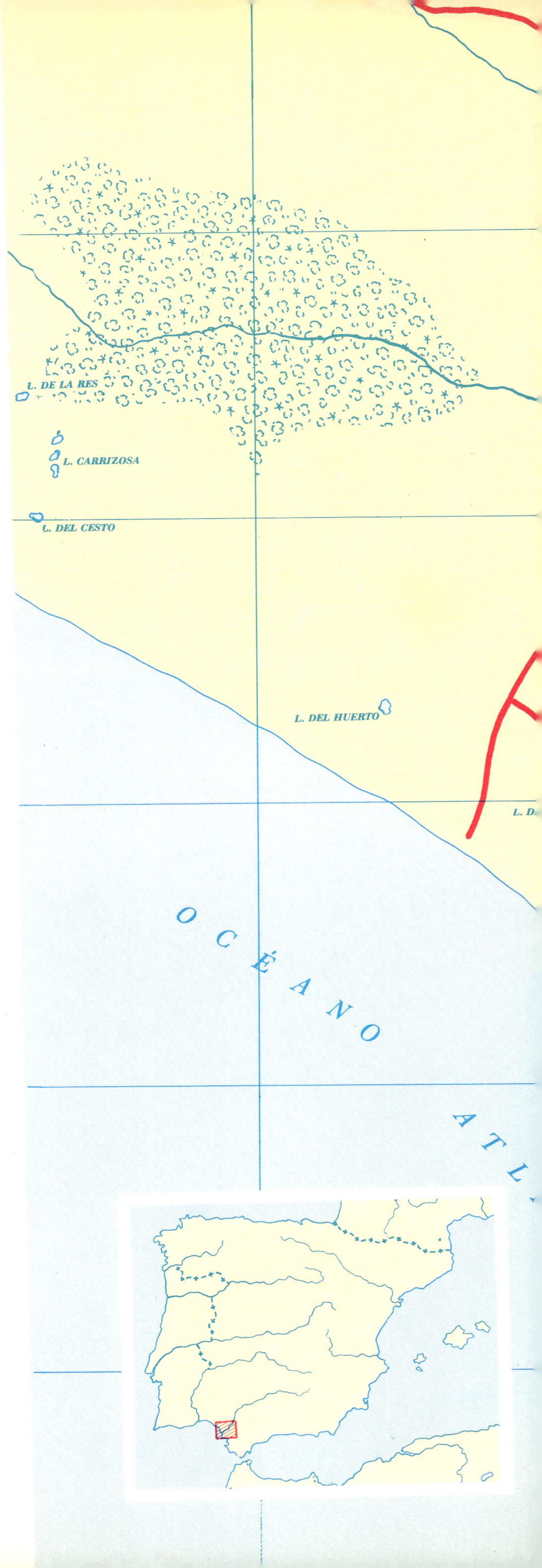

Scrubland

Marshes

Throughout history, Doñana has been a region of variable borders, which were determined essentially by the whims of the kings who hunted there. Although today these boundaries have been fixed by law, Doñana seems to evade legal decrees and the boundaries, though fixed, are in actuality still indistinct.

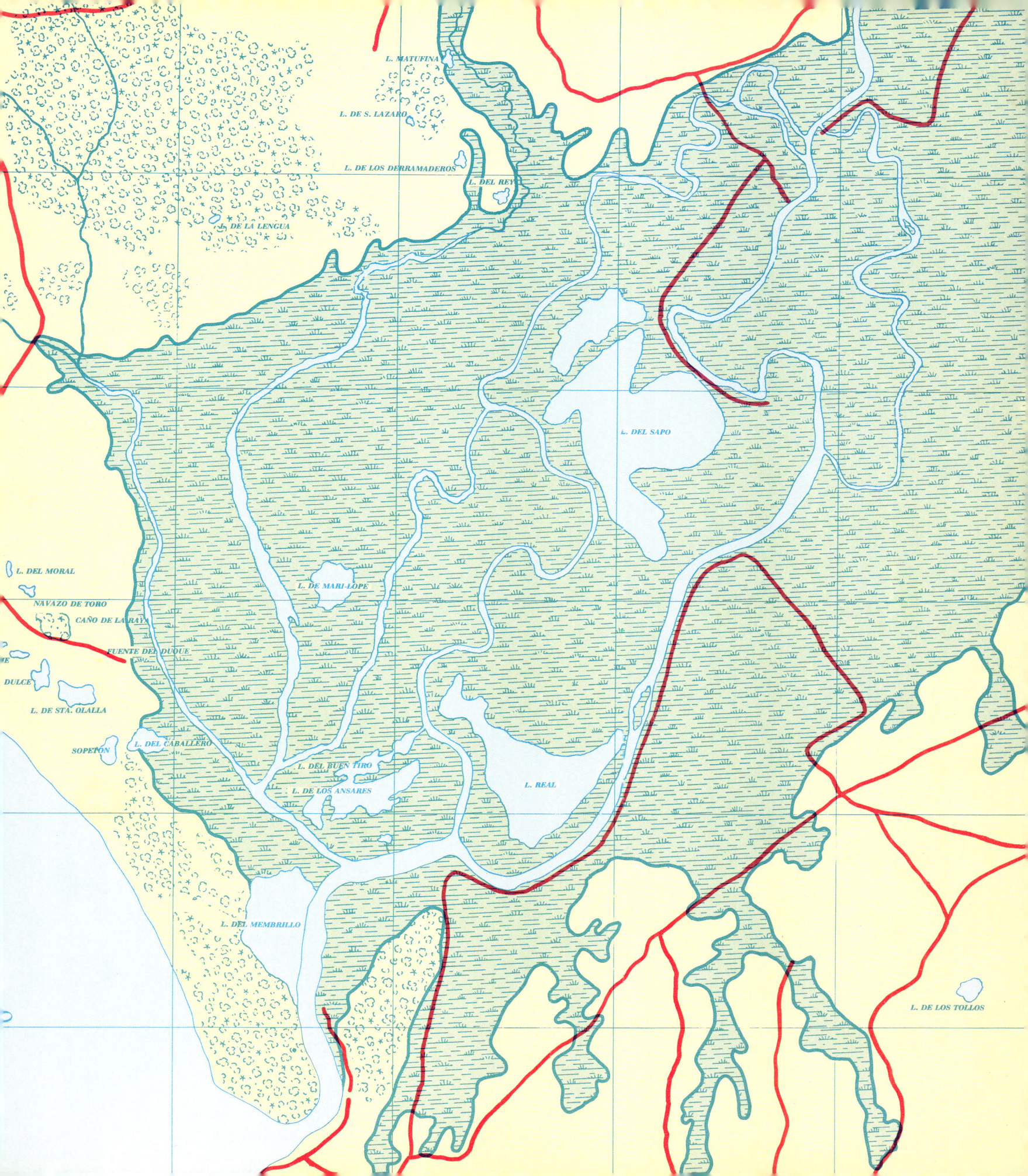

FOREWORD

From the tundras of the north they come, thousands of waterfowl arrowing across the grey skies of approaching winter on the migration flights that will take them to the south of Spain, to what is perhaps Europe's most important bird reserve — the Coto Doñana.

And when winter passes, these same flocks of ducks and geese journey noth again, to breeding grounds in Scandinavia and Russia. Behind the mass exodus from Doñana, their places are taken by other birds — bee-eaters from Ethiopia, egrets from Zaire and storks from South Africa — all of which are attracted to this unique combination of protected pine forests, rolling white sand dunes, and lush green marshes.

Doñana also has a resident population of birds and other animals that are as impressive as are its foreign visitors. The Spanish Imperial Eagle and the Spanish lynx, which are listed in the Red Data Book of Endangered Species, not only live here but survive in today's developing world largely because of the Doñana Reserve. It was established by the World Wildlife Fund and the Spanish government in 1963 and figures as one of the most outstanding reserves named in the Ramsar Convention — an international treaty to protect Wetlands of International Importance.

For those of us who have been privileged to visit the reserve, this book is a vivid reminder of the beauty and excitement we have known there. To readers who have not had such good fortune, it will provide a stunning impression of a paradise — not lost.

Peter Scott.

Few corners of the varied geography of Spain have excited so many persons of such diverse interests as the Coto de Doñana. Lost between the southern coastal sands of Huelva and the arms of the Guadalquivir River, only the marshes of the Camargue can be compared to the fifty thousand hectares of these Andalusian marshes, and its extensive mudflats can only be likened to the 'mader' of the Sahara. However, although Doñana represents the richest and most important natural reserve in Europe, the men who first felt its impact were neither biologists nor scientists. When Felipe IV, Goya or Alfonso XIII made it their pleasure ground, they went not merely to see the marshlands or the different species of fauna that abound there. Alfonso did not visit Doñana over a period of sixteen years simply for the deer he might shoot, nor did Goya choose at random the land that would stamp its imprint on his imperishable work, nor was it by chance that kings of Belgium and empresses of France went there.... There was something more – something far more important. That "something more" can only be the soul of Doñana: the eternal enchantment which bewitches those who watch the dawn over its lakes, see the wild geese flying in winter, or lose themselves in the endless thickets of hearher.

The Glorious Past

Doña Ana Gómez de Mendoza de Silva y de la Cerda

"Near the village of Niebla there is a place called Las Rocinas, which is flat and wooded, and where there are always wild boar— one cannot hunt there except in the spring — winter is too rainy, and summer is too dry and hot." Thus writes Alfonso XI, at some time between 1342 and 1348, in his Book of Hunting.

In the thirteenth century, following the reconquest of the Kingdom of Niebla in 1261 Alfonso X, the Wise, made Las Rocinas a royal hunting ground. Later, in the royal decrees of Fernando the Catholic (1477, 1491, 1494), Carlos V, 1518, and Felipe II, the names of the Royal Preserve and the Royal Forest and Palace of Las Rocinas were given to these exceptional hunting grounds whose imprecise boundaries were determined only by the pleasure of the royal huntsmen.

We know that in the thirteenth century Alfonso X often hunted in the heart of the Coto de Doñana. It is there that the king, because of his deep devotion to the Virgin Mary, erected the Hermitage of Santa Olalla, on the banks of the lake of the same name (1).

The extensive region between Arenas Gorda and the mouth of the Guadalquivir passed to Don Alfonso Pérez de Guzmán by gift of Sancho IV, second son of the Wise King; and later, in direct succession, to the Duke of Medina-Sidonia, whose family possessed these lands for three centuries.

Where documents are lacking, legends arise to take the place of missing facts. These legends are always more colorful than reality, and when written down, tend to become history . Such is the case with the history that we deal with here, and for this reason, it is difficult to determine the

(1) *The ancient remains of stonework, where the house of the guard, Jaime Robles, now stands, are probably the vestiges of this hermitage.*

A fourteenth-century manuscript in which the territory, which today is called Doñana, is mentioned for the first time in a historical document.

exact origin of Doñanas name. But our starting point for this history of the Forest of Doñana shall be a sixteenth century woman named Ana Mendoza de la Cerda, who was the wife of Ruy Gómez de Silva, Prince of Eboli.

The wealthy Princess of Eboli, who was frivolous, indiscreet and capricious, was widowed in 1573. She then spent three restless years in the Carmelite convent of Pastrana, after which she returned to the Court, where she became involved in the deepest intrigue of the reign of Felipe II. Her political designs led her, in league with Antonio Pérez, to form the so-called Ebolist Party and, later, her disloyalty to the crown obliged the king to order her arrest on 28 July 1579. First held in the fortress of San Torcaz, she was later confined in Pastrana, where she died in 1592.

Mistress of Antonio Pérez? Mistress of Felipe II? Given her innate instability and the complicated, intense life she led, both may be true. But legend, which attributes beauty to her irregular features and the passion of love to her smallest caprices, may also have placed her in imaginary, though immortal, beds.

Her daughter Ana, who married Alfonso Pérez de Guzmán, seventh Duke of Medina-Sidonia, was a withdrawn woman and the complete antithesis of her mother. She was scandalized by the tales told to her by her brother, the Duke of Pastrana, and by other members of the Medina-Sidonia family. His account of their mother's licentious life appears to have been the major cause for the steps which the sensitive duchess was subsequently to take.

The unhappy Doña Ana persuaded her husband to leave his rich domain of Sanlúcar de Barrameda and retire to the oak and pine forest which stretched out on the other side of the

A view of the Palace of Doñana: when within these ancient white walls, one recalls the sovereigns of Spain who stayed there and the historical events which took place there.

Guadalquivir River. However, the title to this extensive wild region which had been the royal inheritance of the first Duke of Medina-Sidonia, had since passed to the Council of the town of Almonte (the result of a protracted lawsuit which began during the reign of the Catholic Kings and was resolved only towards the end of the sixteenth century). Therefore, in 1585, the seventh Duke of Medina-Sidonia bought the land — land which had previously belonged to his ancestors — from the Commons of Almonte, and the Guzmáns returned to the southernmost part of their royal inheritance.

Soon thereafter the estate, which followed the coast from Algaida to Matalascañas and bordered the Guadalquivir, began to be called the Forest of Doñana. There, a small palace was built — the Palace of Doñana — in which the woman who gave her untainted and resounding name to an unknown corner of the country spent the rest of her life. As if engraved on the heather and on the sand, the name of Doña Ana survives to the present day, and this remote part of the province of Huelva is now known in naturalistic circles all over the world.

The last years of Doña Ana's life are virtually undocumented. The fanciful pen of legend relates that her sadness was beyond description; that she spent most of her time praying for her mother; and that when death was near she installed herself in a dismal

*Map of Doñana at the end of the nineteenth century. It is kept in the Palace and bears the **barely** legible signatures of Abel Chapman and Walter Buck.*

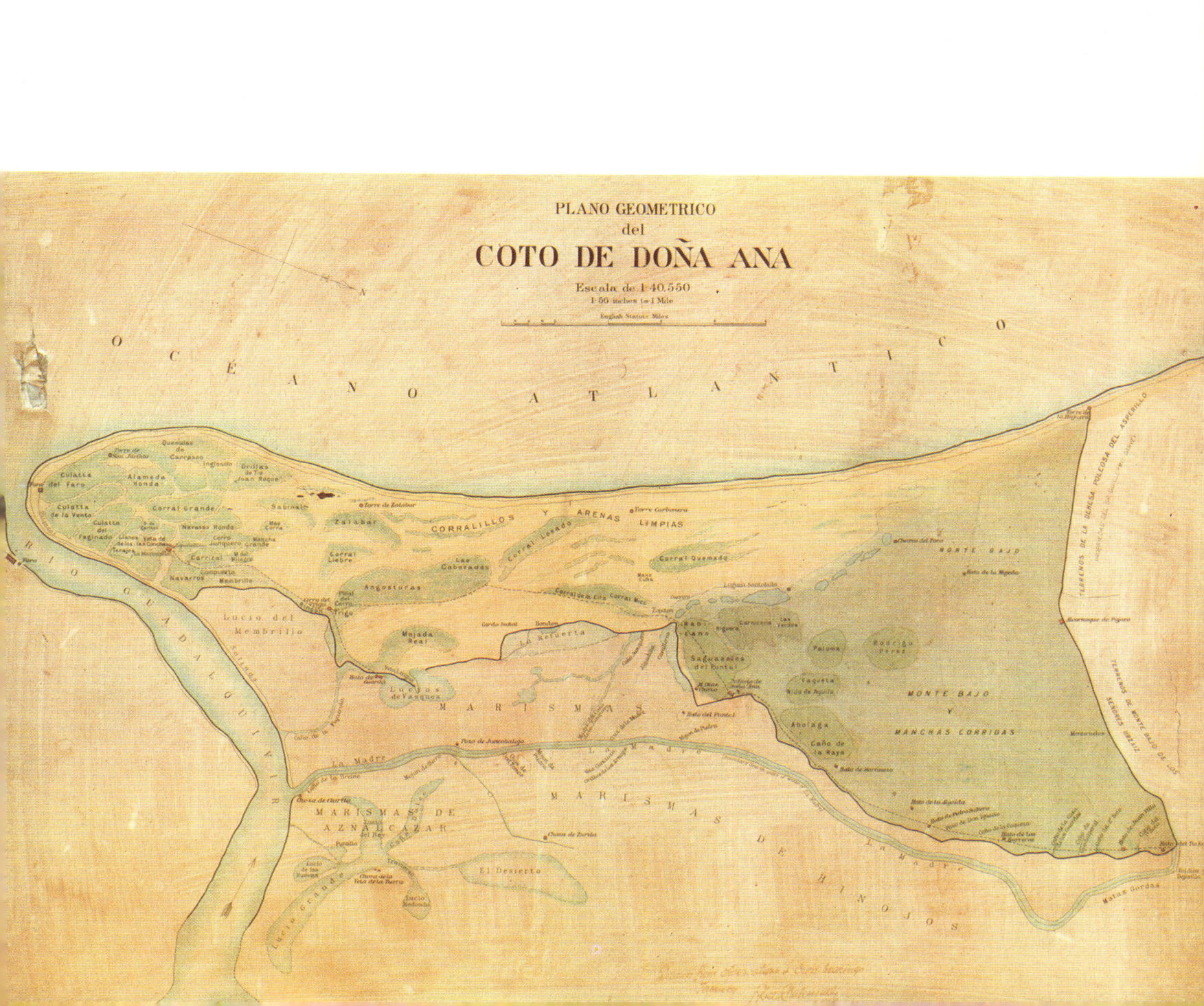

No Spaniard has gained greater praise from the pens of his biographers than the Count-Duke of Olivares, who accompanied the King to Doñana in 1624. Francisco de Quevedo, a great satiric poet, was also a member of that royal party. He wrote in a lighter vein about the powerful minister during those days of pomp and ceremony.

cell in the palace dungeons where she was later joined by her husband.

If her husband had, in fact, joined her in the dungeon, it would not be surprising, considering the life that this unfortunate man had experienced. Poor-spirited, frail, and having a firm belief in his own inferiority, he was destined to be the central figure in one of the most deplorable chapters of Spanish history. Living on his isolated estate in Andalusia, this weak and simple man, Don Alonso Pérez de Guzmán, seventh Duke of Medina-Sidonia, was a true victim of history — appointed against his will by Felipe II to supreme command of the Invincible Armada. The excuses which he proffered the King were manifold, as these extracts from his letters show: "Seasick when I sail"; "Know nothing of the sea or war"; "Only if the king so orders can I undertake that which I know I will be unable to carry out". What happened off the coast of England to that which thereafter was no longer called the Invincible Armada is historical fact. And although the reluctant, defeated admiral could hardly be held responsible by Spain for the disaster, he had sufficient reason for leading a life more and more marked by pessimism and self-contempt.

On the 14th of May, 1610, Doña Ana died in Sanlúcar de Barrameda, where she had been carried in her last hours to receive the rites of her church. She was buried in the pantheon of the Counts of Niebla, in the Church of San Domingo (2). It seems, however, that, in accordance with her last wishes, her remains were later transferred to the Palace of Doña Ana. According to legend, when the Duke died in 1619, by his express command he was buried beside his wife.

(2) *Certified by Deed of Don Cristóbal Bilbao, Public Notary.*

Felipe IV was the great hunter of Doñana. Barrels of gunpowder, lances, horses exhausted in pursuit of the wild boar... all these are described in the chronicles which record the visits of this "weak" son of the House of Austria. Although visited by other monarchs, only centuries later would a king, Alfonso XIII, hunt as frequently and with such pleasure in this Reserve.

In 1902, when work on the interior of the Palace was in progress, a floor collapsed, revealing underground rooms, one of which contained a tomb with neither tablet nor inscription. Inside were found human remains in a very deteriorated state (3). Examinations were made of the remains, but they were inconclusive, and the bones were sent to the ossuary of Almonte.

This stark epitaph is a fitting end to the legend:

"Here, in the white ossuary of Almonte, among nameless bones and broken skulls, bones to which life once clung, lie those who in life were Doña Ana Gómez de Mendoza de Silva y de la Cerda and Don Alonso Pérez de Guzmán, seventh Duke of Medina-Sidonia, Admiral-in-Chief of the Invincible Armada, Captain-General of the Ocean Sea and Viceroy of Andalusia."

(3) *The Palace of Doñana is within one-hundred meters of the marsh, and due to the high humidity, the entire edifice is damp.*

Hunting Parties of Felipe IV

We will never know whether the darts of love or the lances of the chase held first place in the life of Felipe IV, who divided so much of his time between these two activities. For, although the weak-willed Austrian is scornfully described by historians as feeble and contemptible, he was great in one area —the art of hunting.

The journey which the King made to Andalusia in March of 1624 brought him, and his court, to the Forest of Doña Ana, and his visit resulted in the biggest spectacle that ever disturbed those silent lands. The Duke of Medina-Sidonia, anxious to give his sovereign a truly royal welcome, went to such extremes that only the fact that the chronicles of the time agree, leaves no room for doubt concerning their validity. The following extracts from these chronicles will serve to give a partial picture of the preparations made for the king's stay in the land of the Guzmans:

As the day ends, the birds in the Cork Oak Tree at the edge of the marsh fall quiet. It is as if the huge red bell of the sun —pealing for silence— had rung the Angelus.

The mudflats, the desert steppes of the marsh, were from 1829 the habitat of numerous camels. Today a few still survive in the northern zone of the Marisma de los Pobres.

"The Duke sent Don Bernaldo de Morales to the Forest as steward, with 400 men and a great number of beasts of burden, to prepare for the reception of the king...

"To house His Majesty's horses, they built new stables for 200 animals. They erected cabins with a capacity sufficient for 500 persons for the attendants who came with His Majesty, servants and vassals...

"For the kitchen were ordered 80 flasks of old wine, 200 hams of Rute and Aracena, 100 sides of bacon, 400 arrobas* of oil, 600 arrobas of salmon, 50 arrobas of lard, 300 cheeses of Flanders, 1,000 barrels of olives, 100 arrobas of sugar, 100 of sugar loaves, 50 arrobas of honey, 8,000 oranges, 3,000 lemons, 12 loads of hearts of palm... 500 barrels of pickled fish, another 1,000 which had arrived from Sanlúcar with sole, oysters and bream, and 1,400 barrels of lampreys.

"From Sánlucar they brought 100,000 eggs, and at two leagues from the cabins they kept 600 nanny goats for milk, cream and other delicacies. Every day 6 loads of snow were brought from Ronda on 46 mules.

"The Duke gave orders that all game killed within twenty leagues should be sent to the Forest, and warned that nothing should be hunted within the Forest itself, so that His Majesty should be the better entertained."

The chronicles go on to recount the ceremonial for the reception and the transportation of the royal suite from the right bank of the Guadalquivir to the Palace. They describe the luxury and decoration of the rooms reserved for His Majesty and his retinue, and they detail, day by day, the events, hunting parties, festivities, banquets, and all that went into creating this unique spectacle in

---

* *A liquid measure; or a weight of about 25 pounds.*

which more than twelve-hundred people took part.

Referring to the amorous frivolity of Felipe IV, Gregorio Marañon writes of 'the continuous round of affairs with women and more women, high and low, of all moral, social and aesthetic categories" But if he was indiscriminate in his amours, his dedication to hunting was complete, and Felipe IV hunted whenever he wished in Doñana. He lanced wild boar, often ruining his horses in headlong gallop; he hunted flamingos and wild duck from a barge on the lake of Santa Olalla; and he killed deer and wild cattle. His obsession with hunting at Doñana was such that there may be some truth to the legend about a cross which is still to be seen on the left side of the Palace. According to this legend, the King, in discussion one afternoon with the Count-Duke of Olivares and Don Francisco de Quevedo about the range of his harquebus, swore to its strength as he pointed to a servant who was passing nearby with a pitcher of water, declaring that with his weapon he could kill the man, even at such a long distance. The Count-Duke, taking up the harquebus, said that he was willing to shoot, as he would certainly not be able to hit the servant. The King told him to aim carefully, since he would assume full responsability. The Count-Duke did, hit his target, and by that act the intelligent Don Gaspare won the lasting affection of his young sovereign.

Goya paints in the Palace of Doñana and the Empress Eugenia de Montijo spears wild boar in the marsches

Kings, empresses, men of universal renown —their visits are the milestones which mark the proud history of these lands.

At the headquarters of the Hispanic Society of America in New York, hangs a painting by Goya which is the subject of many controversies which surround the famous majas. It is the portrait of Doña Pilar Teresa Cayetana de Silva y Alvarez de Toledo, Duchess of Alba, and is dated 1797. The background depicted in the painting appears to be the Doñana helianthemum in the spring.

At that time, the estate was the property of the Duchess of Alba, who had retired there after the death of her husband. In 1797 she was visited by Goya who, according to even the most serious historians was her lover. After a great deal of research there remains no doubt that this portrait was painted in Doñana (1); and since it is certain that the painter and the duchess lived at the Palace that spring, it would certainly be odd had Goya not chosen that setting in which to paint his beloved model.

(1) *José Goyena, the celebrated Sevillian collector (who for many years owned the portrait originally from the collection of King Louis Phillipe), affirms that this is so. Beruete is in agreement, even going so far as to identify the typical fine background of the work in the style of Corot, with a corner of the helianthemum beside the lake of Santa Olalla.*

Scientists and lovers of the chase are not the only ones who have been entranced by Doñana. Goya, universal giant of painting, brought his palette there in the spring of 1797, and used for a setting the Elysian banks of the Lake of Santa Olalla to paint his immortal model, the Grand Duchess of Alba.

One of the main reasons for the renown of Doñana during the first quarter of this century was the presence of King Alfonso XIII, who was a frequent visitor over a period of sixteen years.

However, the most controversial dispute is over the relation between the maja of New York and the two magnificent paintings in the Prado Museum. Were the Prado majas also painted at Doñana? Some researchers agree that the model and the dates are the same for all three paintings. Perhaps, though, it is better to leave the question unanswered, so that once more the unknown reality might remain and live on in these lands which seem to have been made to immortalize certain deeds and men.

In October 1863 another famous woman, the Empress Eugenia de Montijo, attracted by the legendary fascination of Doñana, visited the preserve in the company of the Princess Anne Murat. Mounted on a thoroughbred, the Empress participated in a spear hunt for wild boar, and soon this delicate lady —surely the most beautiful of Spanish and the most imperial of French women— gained enthusiasm for the manly sport of Felipe IV.

An article appeared in "Le Monde Ilustre" of the 14th of November 1863, describing the arrival of the Empress in a French warship off the coast of Andalusia. The following is an extract from this article:

"The group was formed by the Empress, the Princess Anne, and some persons of their suite, the Duke of Fernandina, the Marquess of Alventos, the Marquess of la Granja...

"They had just come upon a herd of wild pigs. One of the hunters charged the most ferocious, knocking it down; in a moment it was up, and the Duke of Fernandina, who had just arrived, speared it, wounding it mortally; but the beast seemed to have seven lives, and it attacked the Marquess of Alventos, who received it on his lance and held it. The Marquess, seeing the Empress galloping towards the struggle, held off the animal as a picador does a bull, so that Her Majesty could get there. Unluckily, the beast turned and attacked the horse of one of the other hunters, who prepared to receive it with his spear. But the lack of room to maneuver hampered him, and he was unable to prevent his horse from being wounded by the boar's tusks..."

Many lines later the writer ends by averring that the wife of Napoleon III would never forget her journey to Andalusia, the land of her birth.

Alfonso XIII; Constant Hunter at Doñana

In 1897, Don Guillermo Garvey bought the Doñana preserve from the Count of Niebla a transaction which, for the ducal house of Medina-Sidonia, meant the loss of lands traditionally theirs since the fourteenth century when the first Guzmán distinguished himself in the glorious defense of Tarifa.

It was probably during the seventeen years when the preserve belonged to the Garvey family that hunting reached its period of greatest importance. During that time, it was rented by the so-called "Scribes" (Pedro Gonzáles de Soto, Walter J. Buck, Abel Chapman and Alexander Williams) with whom Don Guillermo Garvey and his nephew, Patricio Garvey y González de la Mota, became associates. For a description of the animal life found in Doñana at that time, we quote from Abel Chapman, one of the greatest hunters of his era —and perhaps of any other time— in his works *Wild Spain* and *Memories:*

"Here in spring, in an ornithological Eden, one sees almost daily new bird forms. During the vernal migration the still air resounds with unknown notes, and many of those species which at home are the rarest —hardly known save in books or museums— are here the most conspicuous, filling the desolated landscape with life and animation.

"The months of February and March witness the withdrawal of most of the winter wildfowl. Day after day the clouds of Pintails and Wigeons, of Shovellers, Pochards, and Teal, and fresh files of grey geese wing their way northwards; while their places are simultaneously being filled by arrivals from the South.

"To us, this same Coto Doñana had always appeared as if it were a fragment of some savage African solitude, detached and specially dumped down for our personal benefit in this remote corner of Europe.

"Still for ourselves, hunter-naturalists and lovers of the outer wilds, Doñana represented nothing less than an earthly Paradise..."

In 1912, on the death of Don José Garvey, who had inherited the preserve from his brother Guillermo in 1909, one part of Doñana went to Doña María Medina Garvey, the wife of the Duke of Tarifa. Doña María bought the rest of the preserve for one and one-half million pesetas, and the entire estate thus passed to the Dukes of Tarifa.

During this family's ownership, Doñana experienced a new era of splendor. Hunting was only one of the attractions which the estate held for the Duke, and he took a serious interest in various other activities. He built the Marismilla Palace and, to provide easy access to the preserve from the Guadalquivir, he constructed the pier of La Plancha. The old Palace of Doña Ana was restored and enlarged, and a chapel, dedicated to

Doñana is populated by a wealth of wildlife. It is as plentiful in the inland "vetas" of the marsh as in these "corrals," close to the sea and almost buried by the dunes.

Las Rocinas, which Alfonso X made a Royal Hunting Preserve in the thirteenth century, continues to shelter a treasure of fauna.
Where the vegetation disappears and the shallow waters of Las Rocinas open out towards the marsh, the local men still fish for eels in the most primitive way.

our Lady of Carmen, was built in its inner patio. The Duke's interest in hunting led him to introduce the fallow deer, which adapted itself perfectly to this habitat, and they thrive there today. He was not so fortunate, however, in his similar experiment with ostriches. But of all his innovations, surely the most important was the archaeological research carried out in Doñana during those years, for the Duke subsidized the cost of the excavations made in search of the legendary city of Tartessos.

Tartessos was the name given by the Greeks to the mysterious place where the Phoenicians obtained precious metals. The Greeks had heard of this land in the Far West at the mouth of the Betis where, a thousand years before Christ, a great culture had flourished. The reputation of this empire at its apogee was such that, through the reports of Herodotus and Anacreon, it came to symbolize the height of peace, happiness and good fortune to the ancient Greeks. The site of the capital of this empire, however, has never been discovered, and now only beautiful poetic myths, which include dynasties of gods, give substance to the empire of Tartessos.

Adolf Schulten, a German archaeologist well-known for his work in Italy, Africa and Greece, was the man who began the search for golden Tartessos. Although inconclusive, the excavations made in the Cerro del Trigo, near the Zalabar tower, at least brought back to the fertile heart of Doñana memories of what may have been a glorious past.

The brilliance of Doñana during its ownership by the Duke of Tarifa was largely attributable to his frequent and strictly controlled hunting parties. These were hunts at an aristocratic level, attended regularly by Alfonso XIII over a period of sixteen years. In describing one of them, Don Alfonso Domínguez Domínguez, the King's hunt assistant, writes:

"In the hunt of 25 January, 1924, I was appointed assistant to His Majesty. When my father presented me to him, the King complimented me on having the same name as he, and asked me many questions. Since I told him that I had served in the artillery, whenever he called me he always used the name 'Artillery'.

"I still remember the game shot on that hunt: 83 stags, 42 young boars, 15 fallow deer and 3 lynxes... First came the big game, and then the fabulous duck and wild goose shoot in the marshes. Sometimes there was hare coursing, and partridge shooting in the thickets. But the King also enjoyed watching certain sights of the preserve: the thousands of ducks flying back and forth over the river, the marsh and the lakes; and the number of vultures gliding in tight circles as, after having caught the scent of some dead cow or horse, they prepared to land and gorge on its flesh."

From every corner of Spain pilgrims make their way to El Rocío. From the closer towns of Huelva, Seville and Cádiz they come at the slow pace of ox and cart, opening their own paths over untamed land. They advance unhurriedly, free from the noise of motors, with hearts full of peace and faces radiant with pleasure, attested to by their songs and laughter

El Rocío

Las Rocinas, the first recorded name for what is now Doñana, dates to the time of Alfonso X, and the shrine of El Rocío and the annual pilgrimage thereto have served to provide a continuous historical thread which runs through all of the epochs previously mentioned: from the year 1275 (when Alfonso X ordered the first hermitage built at El Rocío) through the twentieth century, the monarchs and princes who visited Doñana for sport and hunting all prayed there.

The hermitage was dedicated to the Virgin of El Rocío —Holy Mary of Las Rocinas— and the actual image of the Virgin, a thirteenth-century Gothic carving, is dated from the last quarter of that century. It is only legend, however, which tells us that the image first appeared long ago among the brambles of Las Rocinas.

Drummers of the Brotherhood of Triana from Seville salute the dawn in the classic manner of the Rocío pilgrimage. The Sevillians say that Triana is capital of the world of wit. Perhaps this is true. At least these pipes and drums sound a most joyful "good-morning".

The soul of Andalusia comes alive in heart-felt fervor when the Virgin of Rocío —the White Dove, Queen of the Marshes— appears.

The devotion to the Virgin of El Rocío, which is also widely known as the White Dove and Queen of the Marshes, has spread with time so that today, besides the brotherhoods in Andalusia which make the pilgrimage, there are even brotherhoods in far-off Madrid and Barcelona.

There has always been a close bond between Doñana and this pilgrimage, because several of the brotherhoods must pass through the Reserve en route to El Rocío. These processions, a fanfare of beauty and color, combine a fervor and a gaiety which rival the beauty of Doñana in the spring. The multicolored decorations of the wagons, the artful trappings of the oxen, the beautiful stallions of Jerez and the traditional Andalusian dress of the men and women, all combine to create a radiant and joyful spectacle.

These cavalcades work their way slowly through wild Doñana —across bright meadows of lavender and shallow pools and streams, through dim, shadowy pinewoods where the ground is blanketed by soft, dry needles, and around larger lakes of still water. The tall spikes of gorse sway gently aside to make way for the passage of these splendid caravans which provide such striking contrast to the serene beauty of Doñana— the beauty which is its very essence.

The Biological Station of Doñana

The Duchess of Tarifa, who inherited the preserve from her husband, died in 1933, and after a long legal dispute it passed to her sister, Blanca Medina y Garvey, wife of the Marquis of Borghetto.

A few years later, in 1940, 16,000 hectares of the northern part of the preserve were sold to the Marquis del Mérito, Don Manuel González Gordon, and Don Salvador Noguera Pérez. Their purchase included the areas of Santa Olalla, Palacio, Mogedas, Algaida, and Casa de los Guardas. The Venta, Las Marismillas, Cerro de Trigo, and Veta Lengua remained in the possession of the Borghettos. The three new owners formed a society called the Coto del Palacio de Doñana, a society whose primary interests concerned the game of the preserve.

In 1953 a new era began for Doñana, and scientific interest on an international scale began to take the place of the hunting which had been so dominant throughout its history. At this time, the first scientific publications on Doñana appeared. These continued, growing in importance, a favorable prognostication of future developments. In 1957, a scientific expedition which included some of the most prominent figures in the field of biology (among them, Julian Huxley, holder of a Nobel Prize for Biology) set out to document what was already well known in Spain: the hunting grounds of kings and princes had the potential to become the greatest biological reserve in Europe. International societies for the protection of wildlife —some of which were born of this great endeavor, and others which were strengthened by it— took the project very seriously Under the energetic leadership of the man who was later to become its director, news of the expedition attracted worldwide attention, and was reported by the press in Madrid, Geneva, Paris, London and New York.

The problems associated with setting up a permanent research facility and reserve at Doñana aroused a great deal of interest, a factor which helped to overcome enormous difficulties. On the 30th of December, 1964, the Higher Council of Scientific Research, with financial assistance from the World Wildlife Fund, bought land to establish the Biological Station of Doñana. At the head of this station was placed the man who had fought to bring it into existence and who was now charged with giving it form. This man is Doctor José Antonio Valverde of Valladolid, a man of Castile enamored of the Andalusian marshes.

On the gilded water of Santa Olalla, the Flamingos with their slow, elegant movements enhance the quiet beauty with their ebony silhouettes.

The National Park of Doñana

1969 was a decisive year in the history of Doñana. It was during that year that two developments, occuring almost simultaneously, helped bring to a successful conclusion the tremendous efforts being made to save once and for all —as was then believed— the fauna in what could be Europe's most valuable national park.

The Biological Station of Doñana, with its 6,794 hectares, constituted the minimum possible area for use as a reserve for fauna scattered over more than 100,000 hectares. However, since hunting would be prohibited, those species whose only predator was man would multiply freely, upsetting the entire biological balance.

There were many problems associated with the Reserve. For instance, the access road to the Palace, running for 11.5 kilometers from the highway between El Rocío and Torre de la Higuera, had to be traversed very slowly to avoid "traffic accidents" with the wildlife of the Reserve. The shy, elusive lynxes (which the old guards always spoke of respectfully and in the singular: "That morning, coming by the edge of Cuatro Piernas, I saw the lynx...") were now so numerous that their hunting and breeding territory extended well beyond the borders of the Reserve. In summer and early autumn the red deer, the fallow deer, and the boar wandered many kilometers outside the boundaries. And in winter, at the height of the hunting season, large numbers of wild ducks and geese gathered in the few hectares outside the Reserve which in Doñana afforded them suitable conditions.

Then, as if by two successive miracles, the situation was saved. In May, 1969, enough money was obtained to purchase 3,214 hectares in one of the most important parts of the marshes: the beautiful area of Mari López. In August of the same year, the Council of Ministers passed a decree granting the National Park 35,000 hectares of land which, ornithologically, are perhaps the most valuable in the world.

In 1965 the hunting grounds of kings and princes became an immense natural laboratory. With the creation of the Biological Station of Doñana a new era began; one in which scientific interests would take precedence over the purely hunting ones which had until then been dominant during Doñana's long existence.

Corrals and Dunes

Doñana begins at the sea, where the waters of the Atlantic die on long beaches of fair sand. Then come the undulating white dunes and the corrals. Lakes next appear among green pinewoods, followed by scrubland with seemingly infinite horizons to where it joins the marsh. At last, further still, Doñana ends in fresh water in the curved, many-armed embrace of the Guadalquivir.

The call him "El Pato" (the duck) because he was born at the edge of the sea, and today he uses his nets and fishtraps the same way as his grandfather was taught to use them a century ago. "El Pato" at the seaward edge of Doñana is the first symbol of a distant past; a man who still lives in isolation among the cries of the gulls and the murmur of the sea.

Doñana starts at the sea. Then come white softly-rounded sand dunes. Beyond these are the "corrals": green pines, imprisoned and being buried by the soft sand. And then, like fields of crosses, there are the dry skeletons of dead pines—victims of the sand. Further on come the dense, extensive pinewoods, followed by both small and large lakes, then endless, clear green brushwood... and then the marsh itself, its horizon lost in the distance. Beyond all this, hidden in remoteness, is the winding Guadalquivir River—the ancient Betis—which embraces the marsh before it empties into the sea.

Doñana is bordered by the capricious waters of the Guadalquivir to the south, and is fronted on its western side by the Atlantic Ocean where, for many kilometers, the sea washes upon a beach of fine sand. This beach, extending from Mazagon to Malandar Point where the wide, brown Guadalquivir meets the sea, has been almost untouched for centuries. Torre de la Higuera, Torre Carbonera, Torre Zalabar... these are names from the distant past, names of corroded lighthouses spaced along a forgotten coast.

The huts of the Matalascañas, which are newly built of dried reeds every summer, only add to the wild and desolate aspect because of their primitive architecture. When autumn brings the first tinges of grey to the skies, the reed village is pulled down and the voices of men are no longer

The "coquina" is a delicious mollusk collected in the old manner on these coasts. The fisherman walks backwards stirring up the sand with his feet so that the coquinas, covered by only a few centimeters of sand, are brought to the surface, where they are collected with the rake and dragnet tied to his belt.

heard. The beach is left to the gulls and the sea.

There is one man, however, whose footsteps the waves continue to smooth away summer and winter, when the sun burns and the east wind freezes. This lonely, singular man was born there, his home is there, and there he makes his living. They call him "El Pato."

One day I went to see him. From his hut, with its roof of flattened tins, came the smell of the sea, of fresh fish grilled over hot coals. There was no ceremony: he offered me a seat made of pieces of cork salvaged from the ocean and a glass of local wine. We talked of fish and nets and things of the sea. Night closed over us as the glowing coals of a fire roasted the last fish and El Pato continued to talk of his life, of dolphins stranded by the waves, of giant turtles, of a harpooned whale... When I rose to leave and shook his hand, I felt how hard the sea had made that hand, and saw again the peaceful gaze of that simple fisherman.

At the edge of the sea the sand is littered with flotsam, pieces of net, dead fish covered by dried seaweed, wood: a jumble of useless things. Sometimes a pair of plovers will use this area as a nesting place, the rubbish furnishing protection for their nestlings. Here the sand, scattered with mollusk shells, is yellow as though always wet, and occasionally there can be seen outcrops of hard, red clay. This diverse appearance is characteristic of only a narrow strip which extends some fifty meters from the water's edge. The landward edge marks the beginning of the finest, whitest sands to be found on the Atlantic coast —sands which appear and disappear in a slow relentless advance, as the ridges of their white dunes carry into the very heart of Doñana (1).

(1) *The coast of the province of Huelva, between the mouths of the Guadalquivir and Guadiana Rivers, has a fringe of coastal dunes one hundred and twenty kilometers long and a maximum of eighteen kilometers wide, and has no equal on any other Spanish coast. The fineness of the sand, and the fact that the coastal strip is almost deserted along its full length, are the main reasons for this*

In the background the sky and the sea. Then come the first dunes, enclosing a pine grove. And here, closer to us, is the sand which has smothered a group of pines. Their dry trunks are all that remains.

Shifted by the constant sea breeze, the almost invisible grains mount up little by little —their only impediment the scattered barilla bushes— and by slow, insistent growth the dunes are formed: seemingly endless dunes which resemble the waves of a motionless white sea. Only the pale green fronds of the barilla, swaying in the breeze, break the purity of these beautiful white hills.

After crossing the first dunes we come to those strange depressions which in Doñana are called corrals. The corrals closest to the coast are made up of pine saplings growing unprotected in the grassy soil, where the shade from the taller, mature trees scarcely reaches. Passing among these incipient pine trees, the last green needles still brushing our shoulders, a new landscape suddenly opens up before our eyes: we have reached the "fields of crosses." Over a wide area of flat, unmoving sands the remains of dead pines rear up, the lifeless wood-like burnt fossils— carved by the wind into strange shapes. Some are small and stunted; others, standing on mounds of darkened sand, raise their weathered branches to the sky like arms of a dying Christ. The dazzling sand which condemned and entombed a once-dense pinewood has now formed a desert, and all that remains of the thick stands of pine that once grew here, are a few skeletal "crosses".

Continuing towards the interior, the sands — always the white sands, smoothed by the breeze — rise up again gently, forming little hills and valleys. Here camarina bushes, their long twisted roots above the ground, grow among the sparse barilla. A little further on, after we have struggled up through the bleached powdery sand to the rounded shoulder of the dune, where it has reached its full height, another pine grove appears below us, surrounded by the sands which have already begun to make it into a new corral.

We are now in the territory of the

Like fine white flour, these sands, perhaps the finest in Europe, fringe the length of Doñana between the pinewoods and the sea.

viper. Although found everywhere in Doñana, this snake is most numerous here. We know from its traces in the sand that it covers a wide area in search of prey. It also remains in this zone for the entire year, but of course the seasonal changes of climate affect its life and habits. In winter, like most reptiles, it hibernates under the thick leafmould in the scrub of the corrals. In the spring, the vipers are most active, and the guards of the Reserve call this period "the race." In summer there is what is known as the "hanging" period. The sand becomes so hot that the vipers climb the trees and remain hanging there throughout the day. This is the time when the danger of a viper's bite is greatest: since the snakes are in the trees, a man is likely to be bitten on the head or throat, thus making the use of a tourniquet impossible.

There are few local people who have not at some time been bitten by a viper, and their archaic but apparently effective remedy is the "viper stone." This stone I had believed to be mythical, until I discovered that all the older guards on the Reserve had one. I had often heard these guards, with their extraordinarily clear memories, begin a story with the words, "My great grandfather told me that, when he was a small boy, his grandfather..." At first I, like any other educated man taught to accept a written fact be-

Between the corrals are small sandy deserts where life —so abundant elsewhere in Doñana— does not exist, not even the smallest bit of vegetation. The powdery sands, smoothed by the Atlantic winds, seem to hold us in a sterile world.

fore accepting a verbal tale, would listen to these stories with a decidedly skeptical attitude. But years of acquaintance with these guards —these men who seemed to be part of a distant age— proved to me that they had good sense. And hearing one of them speak for hours on end without any break in continuity, without once contradicting himself, I began to realize that his logic by its very simplicity was irrefutable....Then when one day, after rummaging in a wooden chest, this same man says, "Here it is. This is a viper stone," then I could not doubt without feeling ashamed.

Juan Domínguez Domínguez, a strong, intelligent old man who was a guard at Doñana in the time of Alfonso XIII, was the first to show me a viper stone. The stone was a blackened rosette of deer horn, rough to the touch as I took it from Juan's large, tough hand. Then his cousin, Juan Robles Domínguez, like an alchemist, explained its preparation. I am able to repeat his words exactly since he allowed me to record them that morning when I visited him in Jerez:

"The stone must be soaked for forty days in egg yolk and vinegar; then buried a moon and a half in virgin earth (the white, clean earth of a spring). t must then be taken from the earth and soaked for another forty days in the same egg yolk and vinegar. Then, in a new earthenware pot, it is boiled in a liter of milk until all the milk is consumed. That is its dressing." He continued:

"The stone thus prepared can only be used once. Then it must be boiled in milk so that it can serve again. Mine has been used three times — once for my son, Juan, and twice for the mother of Antonio Chico."

And Juan, who was born in Doñana and had lived there for seventy-seven years, continued to speak in an absorbed and serious manner. He told

The Plover, so appropriately named "little bell" by the people of the marsh, makes its unprotected nest in slight depressions in the ground —sometimes isolated and at other times in dense colonies. However its eggs, normally three in number, are kept safe by their coloration.
Scattered throughout Doñana, Plovers are found at the most distant ponds as well as by the edge of the sea.

me of the adventures of the lynxes, of hunting in Doñana, of the smugglers on the coast... he gave name after name, and even dates and hours, and all that he told me was from memory. When, for instance, he doubted a date, he would say, "Yes, it was that day, a week after the birth of my son José Antonio, the first day my wife went to the well for water..." And so he went on, recounting from his store of memories.

Let us return to the rounded crest of the big dune. There, a few cones still clinging to them, the topmost branches of the first pine engulfed by the sands can be seen. With the passing of the years all the trees in the grove will gradually succumb. Then slowly the dune will move on, leaving a "field of crosses." And over this field, left barren by the advancing sand, life will renew itself little by little, and young pines will spring up. This cyclic process can readily be observed, for there are areas where up to three successive corrals exist, all in different stages of development.

Descending into the corral we find ourselves in a different world. From the vast desert of the dunes, where the steady breeze sings, we are suddenly in a secluded grove, dim and hushed, roofed by the interlaced branches of the pines which spring up from the rich soil. Under these branches it is like a strange extraordinary vault.

These enclosed, twilit corrals— where the presence of Man seems an intrusion, and where the brown needles cover the ground in a deep carpet— are like mystical churches, beautiful but deserted. Even the wildlife here is more subdued. In the thick treetops, hung with misty green curtains of lichen, the owl sits in silence. The call of the wood pigeon is muted. The wild boar wander soundlessly over the soft earth in search of fresh pine kernels. Only the deer, brushing against the tall bushes of broom, disturb this peaceful harmony.

The short-toed eagle is the most representative and noteworthy bird of the dunes and corrals. With the exception of the imperial eagle, it has the greatest wingspan of all the birds of prey which nest in Doñana. Its biological characteristics are adapted to the unusual habitat where it is found. It is rare — only two pairs are known to live here. This small number, with only slight variations, has been maintained since at least the beginning of the century.

Because of its limited reproduction, this bird was called the "single-egg eagle" before it was classified by ornithologists. This in itself is rather surprising, as the short-toed eagle has none of the feeding problems which have forced other species such as the vultures to reduce the size of their annual clutch.

Its unfeathered tarsus, round owl-

The dunes spill the sand from their crests, smothering the pine groves in their slow but relentless advance.

like head, and great yellow eyes are characteristics which clearly distinguish it from other birds of prey. Its specialized feeding habits are also interesting, for in Doñana the short-toed eagle is primarily a predator of snakes. Its method of hunting, although simple, I can describe in detail, since I have observed it myself. It was in April, and we were eating lunch, partly hidden by a great clump of brambles on the edge of Martinazo. A short-toed eagle hovered some fifty meters above a lightly wooded slope. For about three minutes it remained almost stationary in the air, making only a few short movements forward. Suddenly it dived, pausing briefly in mid-flight only to continue again its earthward rush. It remained out of sight for ten minutes, and then with some thirty centimeters of snake dangling from its beak, it reappeared. We hurried to the scene of the drama. The marks in the sand told the story: a clear trail left by the snake wound between low helianthus bushes; then, in a clearing about ten meters wide, the trail stopped abruptly with signs of an unequal struggle. The eagle had waited until its prey was crossing the clearing before hurtling unerringly down upon it.

From our observation of the nests we have noted that the snakes are swallowed whole, to be regurgitated later for the nestling. Only when the chick is very small or the snake unusually large do the parent birds tear off pieces to feed the nestling.

Sometimes lizards form part of this eagle's diet and, less frequently frogs and birds. During several days in December, 1967, opposite the Palace of Doñana itself, we watched a pair of adult birds and a younger one about a year old. This was an unusual observation, for the short-toed eagle is a migratory bird, and normally spends the winter in Africa. However, since that family was living in Doñana at that time of year, snakes were

Although its preferred habitat is the area of dunes and corrals, the viper is numerous throughout Doñana, and is even found near the Palace. In my field diary is a note on the 17th of July, 1967 "Latastes Viper in the interior of the Palace. Two in the entrance hall at 16.30. One in the room of an English visitor at 20.00."

Its existence surrounded by secrets and its preparation described in the obscure language of alchemy, this is a viper stone, which many people believe to be mythical, as I did myself. Yet the stone and its curative powers are as real as this photograph.

obviously not their sole diet, for the reptiles were then in hibernation.

Another bird of prey is to be found on the iodine-steeped coast, where the corral gives way to scented pinewoods and the sands make only surreptitious invasions to the edges of the lakes. This is the hobby, the elegant and swift hunter of dragonflies and swallows.

If, from all the years that I have visited and loved Doñana, I were to choose one event which was espe-

cially memorable to me, it would be the life of "Ginesito," that hobby nestling who, during the summer of 1968, starred in a film on the life of a family of hobbies.

On the 15th of July of that year we found a nest of these falcons near the Charco del Toro, one of the furthermost corners of the Reserve, at the center of which is a large, dark lake hidden in the lee of a high, steep, bramble-covered slope and an immense sand dune. Because of the

The corrals always form depressions which in the rainy spring fill with water. The appearance of a flooded corral is like that of a clear oasis, with pine trees taking the place of palms.

For many years a pair of Peregrine Falcons has nested in the coastal dunes of Doñana near the Torre Carbonera. The distinctive form of this bird is in **striking contrast to the uniformity of the sand**.

biological importance of this species we decided to keep the nest under continual observation, beginning that very day. The information gathered was compiled in a scientific work, and a film was made which had a wide circulation. The following paragraphs, written more than six years ago, are taken from the script of that film and illustrate the extent of my dedication to the study of this species:

"On the first day of August two nestlings hatched, and while the parent birds were engrossed in their young, we erected a small blind supported by eucalyptus poles...

"And these were the first shots our cameras took: two little balls of white down, crouching at the bottom of the nest of bare branches... And from the peep-holes of the blind we began to observe the most intimate details in the lives of this family of hobbies...

"When alone together the two nestlings often pecked each other in fun. This game, played by the young

The constant wind has changed the normal open growth pattern of the spiky furze bushes, and made them into compact, conical masses —dense and close— which enables them to survive despite the coastal wind. These solid shrubs, upon which rabbits feed, are so thick that a man can stand on them.

This is the true face of Doñana: fantastic contrast, ultimate surprise. When the sands appear to be a barren wilderness and the dunes seem to be the unmoving waves of a desert, the white sameness is broken by a surge of life in the appearance of the proud, black Spanish bull.

Past the dunes is a lifeless world of light; and rooted in the arid ground, their trunks as if roughly sketched, are the dead trees holding their limbs to the sky like a dying Christ.

of all species, can be dangerous among predators. for because of hunger it can degenerate into fratricide...

"Five days later we made the same journey, a journey which was to become very familiar to us— from the Palace of Doñana to Charco del Toro. But this time an unpleasant surprise awaited us. As we focused our cameras on the nest, we found that one of the nestlings was missing. We never discovered his fate, but imagine that he probably fell out of the nest and was eaten by some animal, since not even his remains were found...

"We noted that the female, which we were now watching, was the less skilled in feeding her chick; she seemed to discriminate little between the pieces of a recently caught bird, and would just as readily present the nestling with the claws as with a piece of breast...

"The behavior of the male, who was possibly older, was quite different. His arrivals were made somewhat warily, and he would tear the food into small pieces — even the dragonflies...

"With the hobby, as with so many birds of prey, there seems to be no obvious dimorphism until, after many hours of close study, small individual traits become apparent...

"By the 2nd of September the nestling was completely changed. Its original sparse, white down had been replaced by a mass of greyish-white plumage, which in the morning light took on a bluish tint. The primary wing, scapular, and retrix feathers had already appeared...

"From within the blind, aided by strong telephoto lenses, we observed the smallest details, both anatomical and behavioral. The nestling remained on its feet for long periods, scratching

Alone, useless, lonely victims of the wind's caprice a few trees remain alive in the valleys between the dunes.

itself and searching for lice. Ginesito, as we had begun to call him, was almost reared...

"In Doñana the same trail is always full of change, but we were always impatient to get to the distant Charco del Toro over those difficult tracks. And week by week, added to our purely scientific interest, we began to feel a growing affection for this species...

"On nearing the nest, only one of the adults was to be seen, which, with its cries and pretended attacks, greeted us as usual...

"From that day onwards there was only one eagle flying over their territory...

Amidst the fallen pine needles in the corrals, where everything seems to be at variance with brightness, the Cytinus flowers, so very Spanish, are like explosions of light.

The Short-toed Eagle is the most representative and notable bird of the dunes and corrals. Its diet consists almost entirely of snakes, which makes it a super-specialized predator. From observations of their nests, it is known that the parent birds swallow the snake whole, and then regurgitate it to feed the single nestling that they have each year. The nestling also swallows the snake whole.

"Although the nestling still had a great deal of white plumage, which it pulled out as it hunted for lice, the brown of the back and head, and the shape of the jaw were now those of an adult bird. It spent the day in performing flying exercises, and one afternoon, when a wood pigeon went to perch close to the nest, the chick drove it off angrily, prompted by its falcon's dignity...

"The absence of one parent bird and the other's neglect in feeding the nestling worried us greatly that day...

"The greatest difference which we noted from the week before was its greater coordination of movement...

"These were the last shots taken of Ginesito. Moments later he flew up high above the pinewood and we never saw him again. But we like to think of him flying free in the sky like his parents, and hunting to live. And perhaps one day, another year, now an adult, he will return to this pinewood, to the solitary Charco del Toro, to obey the inexorable law of his nature."

The Hobby, smaller brother of the Peregrine Falcon, is a diligent nest-builder in the more interior corrals near the lakes. These photographs show three stages in the life of a Hobby, whose family was the subject of a study made during the summer of 1968. Some of this bird's outstanding characteristics are described in the text.

Pines and Lakes

The enormous nest of the black and "white lady of the towers" is always built in the crowns of cork oak or pine trees. Although at the end of the summer hundreds of storks gather in Doñana before continuing their southern migration the nesting population in the Reserve is not large.

In the sixteenth century the Reserve was called the Forest of Doñana; and the House of the Forest is the name used by a chronicler when he described the visit of Felipe IV to the Palace of Doñana. Judging from these names, and from the fact that a great part of the Mediterranean area has been gradually de-afforestated, these lands which today alternate between scrubland and lakes, pinewoods and oak groves, must once have formed part of a vast forest.

Turning from the sea towards the interior, passing the soft dunes, and the silent, shady corrals, other corrals and dunes lead us into the flat country of Doñana. We are now among lakes and pines.

The lakes are girdled by strong old pines, their green branches reflected in the water, making this perhaps the most idyllic part of all the vast Doñana. The pinewood here is extensive, almost unbroken; the few clearings are formed by lakes or by the intrusive sand which, in its whiteness, appears to emulate the now distant dunes.

This long strip of pines, consisting of the moderate-sized Stone variety which never reaches an excessive height, has a most varied undergrowth — at times tall and compact, at other times giving way to large open spaces where only a springy carpet of pine needles covers the ground. Thick, spiky furze springs up

The pinewood of San Agustín, woody entrance to the Palace of Doñana, has no undergrowth. Its red-tinged, bare, straight trunks are reminiscent of the crowded columns in a silent mosque.

among rosemary and blackberry bushes, and tall broom forms green walls measuring up to three meters in height. In spring, the dense bright blossoms of the broom make brilliant splashes against the green foliage and the brown earth. But an undergrowth of medium height is generally found in these woodlands, and the dominant note is one of severity. In the clearings, where the tree trunks rise from the bare earth, the ground is covered with old, empty pine cones, whose twisted bracts look like dead grey flowers worked in blackened silver.

The wildlife of the pinewood is plentiful and varied; birds, beasts and reptiles all use it as a hunting and a breeding ground. All the animals of Doñana, including the wild boar, the deer and the lynx, pass through it in their foraging, the fallow deer being

The sky at sunset.

the creature which inhabits it least. In the strong tree forks nest a wide variety of birds, ranging from the gentle turtle dove to the imperial eagle.

This fringe of pinewood running parallel to the chain of dunes and corrals, which further inland gives way to the scrubland, is all that remains of an extensive forest of cork oaks which existed here in times past. This is demonstrated by the fact that the entire scrub region of Doñana is dotted with both small groves of pines and small-to-medium stands of cork oaks. The lack of firebreaks has meant frequent devastation by forest fires. The last of these destructive blazes started on the 8th of September, 1947, and ironically the eleven-year-old boy who accidentally started

In the clearings between the pines, where there is none of the leafy undergrowth which in other areas is almost impassable, there are mounds of pine cones which have yielded their sweet contents to the wild boar. Now, their bracts grey and twisted, they pave the seldom-trod ground.

In the thick pinewood the Azure-winged Magpie lives and nests. It is rare to see one alone as they normally live in colonies, sometimes very large.

it, Don José Boixo, is now the Senior Guard at the Biological Station of Doñana.

Paralleling the coast beyond the dunes and the pines is a complex of lakes... many of which are shimmering pools having an almost ethereal quality. Others, with the same boldness as the white sands, appear in the heart of the woodland, breaking the continuity, as if wanting to lessen its severity and vastness.

Never did water appear so bold; never did a lake take on dimensions of such beauty, nor have its true meaning fully realized, until seen in Doñana where it becomes a symbol of peace among the pines.

Giving the impression of wishing to please all individual tastes, the lakes of Doñana are varied even in the color of their waters. Charco del Toro has mysterious black water; Taraje in summer is edged with mauve-colored silt. Santa Olalla is green and, when whipped by the sea wind, flings emerald foam on its eastern bank.

Santa Olalla is the big sister — huge, steeped in history and legend. The name goes back to the thirteenth century, when Alfonso X raised a hermitage on its bank. The lake's history continues with a visit by Felipe IV, who took part in the greatest aquatic bird hunt of the time on these waters. Below is an extract, taken from a detailed contemporary account which describes the hunt:

"Later he returned to the lake of Santa Olalla, where the Duke had ordered a punt and three skiffs to be prepared: the punt to carry His Majesty, its stern gilded, bow, sides and oars painted green, lined inside with watered silk of the same color, and adorned with gilded rails and studs. The rowers were dressed as sailors, their jackets and wide-bottomed trousers, jerkins, stockings and garters all of green. In this punt sailed His Majesty, the Count of Olivares, the Count of Niebla, who was in command, and two crossbowmen charged with the care of His Majesty's arms...

Lake Taraje owes its name to the many large tamarisks which cover its southern bank. In winter its broad waters shelter numerous ducks of many species. At the beginning of summer, when the marsh dries up, duck, coot and grebe in incredible numbers find in its dwindling waters a lifesaving redoubt.

The cattle which live in the interior of the scrubland near the lakes have been wild for centuries, and are perhaps the most dangerous animals in Doñana.

Towards the end of the summer Lake Taraje usually dries up. The water, tortured by the pitiless sun, escapes from its green-banked prison, the winged inhabitants abandon it; and its lakebed is covered with strange, mauve-colored silt.

"He killed many birds and became such an enthusiast of this sport and of the lake that on various occasions he remarked to the Count that never in his life had he enjoyed himself more..."

It is difficult to picture this spectacle of color, pomp and noise disturbing the silent clarity of Santa Olalla. May the privilege of profaning it be only for kings.

But the generous beauty of the great lake lies not only in the attractions of its game. In 1797, when Goya painted the Duchess of Alba, he chose as background the verdant banks of Santa Olalla.

In distinct contrast to the rest of the lakes in the area, Santa Olalla is the only salt lake. The oddity is accentuated if we consider that other lakes, such as Dulce — thus called because of this very discrepancy — are so close to Santa Olalla that in a year of high water their waters merge. This salinity permits the existence of certain shellfish that form part of the diet of the pink flamingos and give the wings of these birds their crimson color.

The numerous and varied fauna of Santa Olalla is particularly rich in aquatic birds which, during the harshest months of the year, live on these temperate waters and form such compact masses that they cover almost the entire surface. The mallard, teal, pintail, pochard, as well as many other species of duck, both native and migratory, inhabit the marsh, spending parts of their lives on the great lake; and at dawn and dusk they are to be seen flying across the rose-tinted sky from marsh to lake.

The flamingos, those languid hook-beaked aristocrats with their thin necks and legs, fill the water with color and make the sky seem to sway with their slow extended flight. Their curved silhouettes, moving gracefully through the waters, are like symbols of peace.

To describe this great lake, carved out of the dark woods and the refuge of many-hued birds, is a difficult task for pen and paper. One feels impotent in the face of such overwhelming beauty, and discovers once more the poverty of words.

Few scenes can equal the dawn of day over the tranquil waters of Lake Dulce. The simple daily renewal of life is here seen in its very essence, like a song of praise rising to greet the morning light Years ago I watched this dawn of light and life from a rough wooden hut raised over the waters on pine trunks, like a solitary lake dwelling. I could not keep pent up within me all that I saw and felt, but had to record it, to release that emotion; and on the hard wood of the hut I wrote some lines. I had forgotten them until recently, when I dis-

Seagulls are occasional visitors to the lakes. In the middle of summer, Lake Dulce with its abundant fauna, is often frequented by gulls of various species.

From dawn until evening, the sky over Doñana is filled with wings. In the dim light of evening, a Heron returns to the oakwood near the marsh.

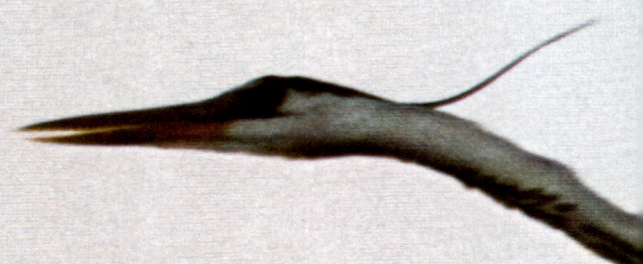

The light and color of a photograph does not do justice to the sight of the graceful bodies of the Flamingos as they take flight and rise above the water. The black and red wings move, the bodies lengthen, the awkward pink legs run in uncertain time, and light sparkles from the splashing water as they stretch their necks forward and lift themselves free from the surface.

are the most typical. However, other small lakes and ponds are scattered throughout the woods and scrubland. Each one, no matter how small, has a name; and some, like the Moral, isolated and hidden, surrounded by ancient oaks, are oases in the harshest part of the Reserve.

Doñana's complex of lakes plays an extremely important role in the ecology of this extensive area (perhaps as much as 100,000 hectares). Without them, the arrival of summer would mean the total disappearance of all the wildlife of the marshes which dry up to become a dusty, arid plain, where water is only the most elusive of mirages. The deer and wild boar require a habitat providing water, mud and dampness; and in general all the fauna of the scrubland require a damp temperate habitat during the hot, dry summer. Only the lakes in the interior of Doñana provide these conditions.

The Spoonbills, which breed in the great "aviaries" in the cork oak woods at the edge of the marsh, fish industriously during the month of August in Lake Dulce. There they teach their young the use of their long, spatulate bills.

When watching this bird, one sometimes sees a curious spectacle. Using its strong beak, it pulls up bullrush shoots, and then with the dexterity of a primate it takes the shoots in its foot and brings them to its beak. Its long claws, the same bright crimson color as its legs, clutch the plant like a monkey's fingers. This is the Purple Gallinule, king of the reedbeds.

Scrubland of Doñana

The scrubland in general terms consists of uncultivated land covered with trees, bushes and shrubs. However, the scientific name for this type of Mediterranean vegetation —Xerophitic— describes this area of Doñana more accurately.

This zone, which extends the length of the northern part of the Reserve, and in the past must have covered vast areas, now lies in a strip of varying widths between the dunes and the edge of the marshes. It is not possible to limit our discussion to the scrubland proper, entirely treeless, since it cannot be separated, ecologically speaking, from the pine woods and groves of oak.

Of the 40,000 hectares of scrub, we shall discuss only the 25,000 which have the characteristics described above. The predominant vegetation is the rock rose, or "white scrub" as it is called locally; but the flora as a whole is sufficiently varied for us to describe it in more detail.

Looking inland from the height of the dunes, we see an endless green plain, its colors pale and blurred, where only the tops of the pines, glistening below us, stand out from the variegated plant life. Here and there, splashes of a more intense green are made by isolated pine groves; the stands of cork oak are grey-green shadows, and light gleams from a solitary lake. But the background to this view is the flat, monotonous dull green of Doñana's scrubland.

As well as ponds and small lakes, there are stands of pines and many isolated cork oak trees which break the severe uniformity of the scrubland and provide shelter for a numerous and varied fauna.

Paradoxically, the rock rose, which is the basic vegetation of the scrubland, is that which shelters the least fauna. However, as we have already said, the scrub proper cannot be separated from the rest of the vegetation, which with it constitutes the area where the wildlife forms a community. Nor can the scattered groves of pine and oak which, although supporting specific fauna, are so intimately related to the scrubland that it would be improper to discuss them separately — for in this close relationship lies the special interest of Doñana's scrub. When this sandy soil, covered in sparse brushwood, appears most arid; when the only thing that moves is a startled rabbit or a snake fleeing our steps; an oak tree, old and twisted, its brown bulk standing among fresh green bracken, rises up at the edge of a clear pool, where wild boar snuffle or a deer bathes. From the branches comes the song of a bird and we, standing below in the leafy ferns, find a cool shelter from the heat of May.

In the slightly lower areas of the scrubland grow impenetrable jungles of heather, reaching as high as four meters, and covering many hectares. They are criss-crossed with narrow, dark paths worn by foraging deer. To traverse these endless, narrow defiles gives one an uneasy feeling of claustrophobia.

At other times the heather is invaded by labyrinthine brambles, their

Usually the deer pass the day hidden in the larger patches of vegetation of the scrubland. Sometimes the questioning eyes of a stag will appear from among the thick bushes, watching our passage.

This Ocellated, or Eyed Lizard, which can kill rabbits in turn often falls victim to the larger snakes which inhabit the scrubland.

long branches wrapped around the thickest patches of scrub like the tentacles of a gigantic octopus. These thickets are incredibly dense, as I once discovered for myself. With the help of two guards I was searching for the nest of a marsh harrier. We had brought a ladder, and on this we climbed to the top of the thicket; then, placing two small planks on the roof of the impenetrably tangled vegetation, we advanced over the strangest floor that I have ever trod. These jungles, which only a powerful bulldozer could penetrate, are the breeding grounds of the lynxes. One thicket in particular, in the area known as Las Verdes, is used every year by the same pair. Although because of the density of the vegetation, it has never been possible to reach the lair, the tracks of the cubs, when they begin to move about, and those of the parents, are noted by the guards; and to these experts they are like reading a book describing the games and tumbles, the fondlings and bustlings of the whole active family.

At times the vegetation of the scrubland is very sparse, and scattered bushes of furze stand rigid in fields of lavender, those sweet-smelling flowers from which essence of lavender is extracted, and which here perfume the land. In other places heavily-scented marjoram grows among delicate bushes of rosemary and the brave green of the savins.

The fauna of the scrubland is numerous and ever-changing. In addition to those species which inhabit it almost exclusively, there are many which, because of its proximity to the lakes and woods, forage or hunt there.

Perhaps the rabbit, found everywhere from the corrals to the marsh, is the most typical inhabitant. It is

All mongooses are agile hunters of snakes, many being immunized against the various venoms. The European Mongoose, which has its most numerous population in Doñana, is also a magnificent hunter of reptiles; however, it prefers to eat rabbits, and occasionally seems to hunt in droves formed by several congeries.

At dusk the deer leave their daytime hides among the densest scrub and make for the open country, where they browse during the night.

most heavily concentrated in the zone of the rock rose, which borders the area of lakes and pools. These likeable little beasts are the prey of many species. When small they easily fall victim to large lizards and snakes, as well as to all other predators. The adults are hunted by the lynx, eagle, mongoose and fox. In scientific terms the rabbit possesses an extremely high rate of Appetite Satisfaction (an ecological term introduced by Valverde in 1962). In other words, the number of calories it supplies when eaten is far superior to the number expended in the effort of catching it.

In contrast to the prolific and frequently seen rabbit, the badger and the mongoose are mammals about which little is known. Of the first, with its nocturnal habits, more has

Between April and May the deer cast their horns, and the new horns are covered in thick skin. During this period the deer become even more timid and wary and hide themselves deeper in the scrub.

been learned about its life in Doñana from tracks indicating its activities, than from direct observation. It lives in long burrows and has a varied, protein-rich diet, including honey, rats and baby rabbits, a large range of insects, grubs and snails, and many bulbs. In its search for worms and other burrowing prey it makes cone-shaped holes in the damp earth, some twenty centimeters in diameter and thirty centimeters in depth, and it also does a great deal of damage to beehives.

I will never forget the despair of a guard in the Santa Olalla district, whose hives had been almost completely destroyed in a few nights by badgers.

The mongoose of Doñana, more correctly called ichneumon, is the most diurnal carnivore of the region. It is found in large numbers in the lentisk thickets of the north and the Marismilla area, and is perhaps more numerous here than anywhere else in Europe. However, the dense vegetation of its habitat means that it is seen only fleetingly. All observations of this animal have one thing in common: brevity. It is therefore not well known, but on occasion, unusual habits have been noted. Juan Boixo, who has lived in Doñana for thirty-one years, told me of having once seen a file of six mongooses, nose to tail, leisurely crossing the scrubland in perfect formation. The above observation, added to the fact that mongooses have been seen hunting rabbits in droves, and added to the high density of the population existing in some parts of the Reserve, seems to imply a certain social character in the activities of this species.

A charming contrast to the shy characteristics of her enigmatic fellows is "Juanita," who lives in the Palace of Doñana. Juanita is an adult mongoose, gay and lively, without the least trace of either timidity or aggressiveness — a gentle creature in these wild lands. When she was so small that she fitted into the palm of a hand, she was found abandoned or lost. Lovingly reared on milk and eggs, and later on her natural carnivorous diet, she prospered. Today, her behavior is the same as that of many household pets. She plays with the children, sleeps in the beds, makes her appearance in the dining room at the crucial hour... until she commits some heinous crime, for which she is punished like a child and banished from the room. But Juanita is no ordinary mongoose: she is a vivacious star who has appeared —to the best of my knowledge— on the television screens of seven European countries.

The largest mammals which inhabit the scrublands are the deer and the wild boar. The latter, although preferring those areas which border the marsh, are found throughout Doñana, searching for pine kernels in the corrals, and foraging in the interior of the marsh when its waters have receded. Although the boar is generally a vegetarian, subsisting on bulbs and roots, it occasionally augments this diet with animal protein. At these

Scattered throughout Doñana are small wells and water holes —places frequented by deer. The paths which they use in their daily movements about the scrubland usually will lead to one of these ponds. Near the water, with the wind in one's favor, in complete silence and with great patience, one can witness unforgettable scenes.

times, its voracity is extreme, and it causes great damage among fauna. In one case, a whole colony of flamingos in the Hinojos marsh was destroyed by foraging boars. I personally saw the devastation caused among a group of purple herons in June, 1967. We had found a large colony of these birds, and when the nestlings were a suitable size we organized a banding expedition. Arriving at the nesting ground, we discovered the nests overturned among a litter of torn feathers, pieces of flesh and dried blood — the remains of what, a few days before, were the nestlings of these courageous, lovely birds, whose enemy is the tusked wild boar.

The deer of Doñana are different from those found elsewhere on the Iberian Peninsula, and their number is quite large — more than 6,500. Their days are passed entirely in the scrubland and they generally sleep during the noon hours. In the evening the deer leave the thickets for the lakes and marsh edges, and at dawn they return again to the shelter of the scrub. Their diet is completely vegetarian, and the amount of rain which falls during the year directly affects

The Magpies are the small-rubbish collectors of Doñana Although they normally nest and live in the heather and brambles of the scrubland, their search for food carries them over all areas. Here we see them eating the soft tissues of a carcass at the edge of the marsh. Later, after the Vultures have opened the skin with their sharp beaks, the Magpies will join the great carrion birds at their feast.

their state of health, which is reflected in the weight of their bodies and the size of their horns. Between April and May the males cast their horns, which are found scattered on the ground in large numbers. These antlers are often found to be gnawed. The explanation is simple: a lack of calcium, most acute in gestating females, caused by the composition of the soil —acidic and siliceous— which some species alleviate by eating the hard, compact deer horn.

The rutting season begins in August, and intensifies in September. At this time the stag lives with his harem of hinds which he has won in sometimes bloody combat. This is a magnificent time in Doñana. As night begins to fall one hears the distant bellows of the stags breaking through the heather in the scrubland. Later, the handsome stags arrive at the dry marsh, and raising their antlers towards the indigo sky, they launch their wild, challenging calls. At night the love calls of these splendid beasts continue to echo around the silent Palace.

One of the greatest spectacles of late summer in Doñana is that of two

The Wild Boar is intensely active at night, and it is seldom seen during the day. At sunset and at twilight it is easily surprised as it comes out to forage in the lakes and marsh. The reedbeds along the perimeter of the marsh are sometimes, on winter mornings, a place to meet these grim-looking inhabitants of the scrub.

fighting stags exchanging powerful blows with their antlers — antlers which are sometimes broken and scattered on the dry, silent earth of the marsh, as a result of the terrible clashes in these fierce duels. They say there is nothing to equal the sight and sound of two stags fighting in the moonlight, but the nocturnal concert alone, heard through the venerable walls of the Palace, is enough. This is the true music of these lands.

Deer have always been the most coveted trophies of the hunters in Doñana — especially, perhaps, during its heyday in the first quarter of this century when the preserve was the property of the Duke of Tarifa. This was the epoch —already mentioned— of the royal hunts, when year after year Doñana and the king paid each other their respects. I have asked Juan Domínguez Domínguez, a retired guard of Doñana, to recount

The Wild Boar has a temperament similar to that of the fighting bull. It avoids fighting, but once it begins, it continues bravely until death. I have seen a boar charge a Land Rover and bury its tusks in the body of the vehicle. Another large specimen weighing ten arrobas (about 250 pounds), killed half a pack of hounds with the slashes of its dagger-like tusks and wounded three horses before it died, pierced by several spears.

The nest of the multi-colored bee-eater in the sand of the scrubland, has long tubular galleries. Their greatest enemy is the snake, which destroys many nests.

The shy Nightjar is one of the least-known birds of all those found in Doñana.

something of these hunts in his own words. He is not an old man—he simply has lived a great many years, and is healthy and alert in mind and body. I encountered him in the fields, at his hives of rosemary honey, that same flower which has perfumed the air all his life (for Juan continues to live in Doñana). He took me to his small house, and with the generosity of the Andalusian country people, he recounted his memories. His gaze is serene and his large, firm hands open now and then, as if to add weight to his recollections. When I asked him about some anecdote he raised these hands slowly to his temples, covered his eyes, mused for a moment, and said:

"It happened that in the re-count I was the one charged with taking notes of each gentleman's bag. Someone tapped me on the shoulder and,

The birds monopolize most of the color of Doñana, for with few exceptions the vegetation —generous only in its magnitude— is devoid of bright hues.

Normally the Wild Boar rests during the day in the thickest scrub and visits the marsh only at night. In the morning it returns sluggishly to the scrub, its belly full after hours of foraging.

thinking it was a companion, I said, 'Leave me alone, man, can't you see I'm busy?'

"But he tapped me a second time, and I said, 'Will you leave me be! Let me finish my work!' Saying this I looked behind me — and saw it was the King! I turned cold, for my way of speaking had hardly been correct. Then I said, 'Excuse me, Your Royal Highness, but I thought you were one of my workmates.'

"The King, laughing, told me not to worry, that he'd come to give his tally, which was four stags and two boar."

Juan has fond memories of his life, and his face is shadowed and sad when he speaks of the King with whom he was in such direct contact in the solitude of Doñana. His wife told me that there are tears in his eyes when he watches scenes from those royal times on television. But he is objective, and when I asked him if this king, whom he revered, was a good shot, he answered without hesitation: "Well, look, he wasn't the best, although he was shooting mad. In the hunt of 26 January, 1924, my brother Alfonso, who was his assistant, told me he found twenty-six empty cartridges in the King's post, and he had only killed three deer. It might have been a bad day—"

In his house in the village of El Rocío we talked much longer, for Juan, even at his age, is a true Andalusian, whose drinking is an art and whose conversation is full of wit.

Of all the birds which inhabit or nest in the scrubland — among which we might describe the stone curlew, which fills the twilight air with its noisy chattering, its cries and lamentations, or the timid nightjar, which remains hidden rather than display its wings— mention must be made of the well-known magpie, if only because it is so numerous. This small member of the crow family, with its long tail and black-and-white plumage tinged with blue, inhabits practically the whole scrubland. Like all the members of this species, the magpie shows a higher intelligence than other birds, and many aspects of its behavior are so unusual that it is the subject of numerous studies. Dr. Alvarez, who is engaged in research on the magpie's capacity of selective rejection of an intruder's eggs, told me of some interesting discoveries. Since the nests of the magpie are used by the cuckoo to deposit its eggs, the magpie has learned to hatch only its own eggs, almost always distinguishing the parasitic cuckoo egg from its own, which are very similar. Most birds lack this ability, and have even incubated —in experimental tests— large wooden eggs considerably bigger than their own. In his attempt to discover what quality or qualities enable the female magpie to distinguish the alien egg, this scientist firmly believes that this bird has a peculiar intelligence of its own.

If the caterpillar is handsome, the butterfly which it becomes is more so. This is the Papilio Machaon, which fills the air over the marsh with color and the feeling of spring.

The water jar is the Andalusian country man's solution to thirst in the heat of summer. The people of Doñana use vessels made of the fragrant clay of Lebrija, which gives freshness to the stream of crystal-clear water.

In the thirteenth century, on the banks of a lake which since that time has borne the name of Santa Olalla, Alfonso X constructed a hermitage where he could pray during his hunting visits to the preserve. The foundations of this hermitage are now beneath the house of the guard of this district, Jaime Robles.

The Unusual Scrubland of the South

The scrubland of the rock rose, mixed with heather and rosemary, and dotted with small lakes and pinewoods, is the typical scrub of Doñana, and covers large areas in the center of the Reserve. However, in the northern and southern parts of Doñana the scrubland is quite different, with marked individual characteristics. In the north, the scrub gives way to tall pines and wild lentisks, and to plantations of eucalyptus. The south is completely at variance with the north and, full of strange beauty, it deserves to be described in greater detail.

The southern zone forms an inverted triangle, with its base on the southern edge of the central scrubland, its apex at the mouth of the Guadalquivir, and its sides formed by the river itself and the Atlantic coast.

One of the main reasons for its divergence from the typical scrub is its narrowness and the more shifting character of its sands, which here, formed into dunes, invade the marsh. Here too, the continuous scrub of the central zone at times disappears in sandy deserts, and at other times is

During the rutting season at the end of the summer this powerful stag will fight, perhaps to the death, and will shatter the silence with its thunderous voice. At other times, in the solitude of the small water holes hidden in the scrubland, it is a symbol of peace.

Among the tortoises, commonly associated with an aquatic life, there are many land species, such as the Greek Tortoise, which is numerous in the scrubland of Doñana.

A small Warbler on its little home.

covered by dense pinewoods. In the center, we are able, with some precision, to divide the terrain into dunes, corrals, lakes, etc., but here in the south we find an incredible geographical anarchy. If an aerial view of this area gives the impression of a complicated jig-saw puzzle (aerial photographs of the region do seem both incomprehensible and absurd), direct contact with the terrain confirms this incoherence. Each step brings a surprise; every hectare is a different color; we never know what to expect beyond the next hillock—water or land, arid dunes or almost tropical forest. The Rincon de Membrillo, which lies in the part with the pools of the same name, is an excellent example of this. Within an area of a few hectares of large dunes, whose fine white sand drifts over the banks of the pools, grow great pines, draped in climbing plants which hang rope-like from the branches. The ground is covered with yellow lilies and great clumps of brambles. Bullrushes, growing in the stagnant pools, are enveloped in gaudy water lentils. A little further on, thick bushes of lentisks reaching a height of four or five meters lose themselves in the dense

woods. Before us lie the pools, with thousands of pink flamingos wading in them, and to our left are the treacherous sands —white, arid and lifeless.

The undergrowth, which in the central zone consists chiefly of the rock rose and as a result is frequently sparse and colorless, is here formed into thick clumps, where immense brambles smother thickets of lentisks. These extensive thickets, shaded by the dense pinewood, form a suitable habitat for the shy mongoose, which in this part of Doñana reaches its highest level of population.

Another unusual feature of these woods is the wild grape, whose vines encircle the trunks of the pines to a height of almost fifteen meters, so that in autumn, ripe bunches of grapes hang from the treetops.

The variations in the terrain cause abrupt alterations in the numbers and types of fauna. For instance, the increase in pine groves means a rise in the numbers of azure-winged magpies, while the fallow deer become more numerous in the bare, open country which joins the pinewoods with the marsh.

Lavender bushes, from which essence is extracted, cover large tracts of the scrubland with their lilac petals.

A logical encounter in these lands so full of life: death.

At the end of August and during the month of September there takes place in Doñana a marvelous spectacle: the "berrea" —the mating of the deer. From early evening until daybreak there is to be heard the terrific, hoarse music of love and war which must be one of Nature's most colossal symphonies.

Ancient Cork Oak Trees

At the present time the Spoonbills in Doñana nest only in the cork oaks, and therefore, often constitute the basic fauna of the great "aviaries".

Today, the cork oak woods of Doñana are fragmented— scattered throughout a large part of the region. These stands consist almost entirely of gigantic, ancient trees with gnarled deformed trunks, sometimes grouped about pools or a small area of open country. At other times a cork oak, clad in centuries-old grey bark, will stand alone in magnificent isolation. However there is a considerable park-like wood of cork oaks in the central zone of Doñana —the area from Palacio to Martinazo —between the scrubland and the marsh. This oakwood bordering the edge of the marsh is one of the most important territories in Doñana for two reasons: its beautiful scenery and the great number of species of fauna that live there. It also constitutes one of the best examples of the border effect, a self-explanatory term often used in biology, which explains the richness of the fauna. For there the animals and birds of both scrub and marsh converge, in addition to those whose natural habitat it is, creating a varied population which includes two-thirds of the species found in Doñana.

Generally speaking, any of the great cork oaks is a potential dwelling for a range of fauna from the lynx to the stork; and in fact dozens of species live and reproduce in the shelter

The silhouettes of these Spoonbills appear against the rose and fawn of late afternoon in a majestic cork oak tree bordering the marsh.

of these long-lived colossi. The strong upper branches support the heavy nests of imperial eagles and storks; buzzards, kites, wood pigeons, turtledoves, magpies, and woodchat shrikes settle on the innermost branches; swarming colonies of spoonbills and herons, with their plumage and droppings, transform entire trees into white mansions; and the lynxes, owls, jackdaws and even bats make their homes in the hollow trunks.

During its very long life, the cork oak passes through several stages, its structure varying according to its age. When fully grown it is massive and leafy, attaining a height of about twenty meters, and measuring as much as a meter and a half in diameter at its base. The majority of the oaks in Doñana are at this stage of development. Later begins the slow decline. The leaves become sparser and dead branches appear. After these first signs of decay, the hollowing of the trunk begins. However, the onset of serility in the tree means the beginning of life there for the particular species which install themselves in the empty trunk, while other species requiring thickly-leafed shelter abandon it. The boles of these trees, becoming gradually hollower, are a refuge for lynxes, wild cats, little owls, and barn owls. Jackdaws also make their homes in the hollow trunks, and labor at filling the hollows with twigs until there is just enough space for the nest —itself an architectural feat.

As more time passes, all that remains of the dead oaks are the bare trunks. But the cavities left by the fallen limbs, and the large central hollows (where I have sometimes sheltered from a storm) are still used by fauna as a refuge. Finally, the heavy,

The ``aviaries'' of Doñana are made up of dense colonies of Spoonbills, Herons and Storks, which in the breeding season occupy entire cork oaks.

grey trunks fall and lie peacefully, like sepulchers, beside their stumps: the decayed, ashy bodies of centuries-old giants.

The state of an oak allows us to estimate to some extent the type of fauna which it harbors. However, certain trees become the crowded dwelling of a particular species, thus diverging from the prevailing norm. The famous "aviaries" of Doñana fall into this category. There are generally two of these: one located on the Calo de la Abulaga, and the other on the edge of Martinazo —both occupied by dense populations of spoonbills and herons.

Life in an "aviary" could be compared with that in a beehive, with one important variation: the order and hierarchy of the hive, established for the benefit of the whole community, is replaced by a strict adherence to the particular interests of each family,

In these "aviaries" there exists a definite system of rank for the individuals of the different species. The Storks always occupy the crown of the cork oak; the Herons congregate mostly on the higher outside branches; the Spoonbills are rather more indiscriminately distributed; The Squacco Herons use the secluded interior branches; and the Cattle Egrets nest on the lower boughs.

The Heron, with its fierce temperament and sharp, pointed beak, is capable of defending a colony from small and medium-sized predators. However, if its nest is isolated, the lack of a communal defense system often renders these attributes useless.

from which we might conclude that life in an "aviary" is somewhat turbulent. And so it is. I have spent many days closely observing the events and incidents in one of these swarming bird colonies, and have noted that the beautiful inhabitants pay a high price for their social security. It seems difficult to explain this general security, since each pair of birds is concerned only with its own welfare. However, it appears that, although this theory is open to question, since each pair of birds which forms an "aviary" has its own distinct territory, the dispersion of these birds throughout hundreds of cork oaks would mean that some pairs would nest in the territory of a family of carnivores, with the result that the nestlings, at least, would sure-

ly perish. But in a colony the danger from predators would be spread over the whole group, and the chance of survival would therefore be statistically higher for each bird.

In 1969, I spent nine days observing the life of one of these communities —La Fresnera in the Martinazo district —and I witnessed both beautiful and terrible scenes. I saw human life reflected in that "clean, white-robed society." At day-break the air was filled with the beating of wings in a sky still tinged with gold, as the birds flew to the nearby marsh in search of small carp. After breakfasting they returned to the oaks with

Each year the birds return to their homes and patiently, following their instinct, begin to reconstruct the nests in which they themselves may have been born.

After lovingly caressing one another in the clear springtime light, father and mother take turns incubating the eggs.

This Squacco Heron on an interior branch of a cork oak seems to be hiding the delicate lace of its feathers.

their crops full, those who had nestlings emptying food into the greedy maws of their young, who in their eagerness would force their beaks right into the parent birds' throats. The adults were engrossed only in their own nest and caring for their young or —in some tardy cases— hatching their eggs. If any nest were temporarily left unguarded, it was robbed of its twigs and sometimes almost destroyed. If a nestling foolishly ventured near another nest, it would be cruelly pecked by the adult birds and possibly even pushed out of the tree, to die between the jaws of the wild boar which, well aware of the number of these incidents, frequented the ground beneath the "aviaries."

There were continual border disputes which arose the instant any bird exceeded the limits of its own property; and these limits were only recognized if they were occupied and defended. There were sometimes cases of infidelity in which the females would copulate with males other than their mates. Theft, removal of nests, conjugal infidelity, respect only for force...

But then came the lovely sunset, and the oak was filled with pure white feathers; the sun slowly diminished to a small scarlet ball, the sea breeze blew inland, and the birds, now weary, ruffled their airy plumes in the golden glow of evening.

The black kites, together with the few pairs of other kites which do not migrate, distribute their territories throughout both pine and oak groves; but the density of fauna in the oakwood which lies along the periphery of the marsh —the border effect—

This is the Spoonbill —the moon-colored bird with orange markings and a crest of airy filaments.

naturally results in a higher concentration there of these birds of prey. Like other non-specialized raptorials, their diet includes a wide range of foods, so they have no difficulty in supplying their nests. The kite preys on nestlings and on young birds, fish and amphibians, young rabbits, reptiles and insects. Those whose territory includes an "aviary" devour a great number of heron chicks which are completely defenseless in their parents' absence, since the adults in the neighboring nests —which sometimes even touch— will look on imperturbably at the gory scene. Young rabbits and adults infected with myxomatosis, also fall easy prey to the kite. Some kites prefer to feed on marsh life, however, principally carp and the nestlings of coot. Sometimes a pair will specialize in a particular prey, hunting it exclusively. I remember one pair of black kites which was

The graceful white Heron's capacity for long flights has been demonstrated by its transatlantic journeys.

Birds bloom like flowers; the nests are filled with innocent flesh, and the great house, the cork oak, is alight with the whiteness of new life.

under observation during a period of sixteen days, and the only prey they brought to their nests were toads.

The kestrel and the imperial eagle —which we will discuss separately— complete the group of birds of prey which hunt during the day in this cork oakwood. However, to this list of feathered predators we should add the jackdaw, which raids the colonies of herons by the hundreds to steal their eggs, making off with the egg spitted on its jet-black beak. It is a peculiar but common sight, the large, greenish eggs being propelled through the air by the wings of these perverse thieves.

Now, bypassing the scattered oak groves which have only a limited range of fauna, let us focus our attention on the great park at the edge of the marsh. There, the massive reproduction which takes place in the

At the end of the day life comes to a halt, and the noisy birds, their plumage ruffled by the sea breeze which now, reaches the interior, stand like white statues in the yellow glow of evening.

spring imparts its effusiveness to the twisted branches of huge trees among the thick, shaded ferns in the undergrowth. Amidst the confusion of wood and foliage, the chaos of nests reaches even to the uppermost limbs where the storks have built their large platforms. From the nests comes the loveliest, most eloquent hymn to life that one could ever hope to hear. Rustlings, murmurs, cooings and twitters —the sound of an underground river flowing in a narrow channel, echoing as if through hollow walls— drift out on the warm air.

With the arrival of summer, the noise of new life rises to a crescendo, and the crowns of the cork oaks seem to be covered with living snow. These are the young of the spoonbills and herons, a triumphant symbol of the perpetuation of their species. But one day soon these little white balls of fluff, now flirting with the grave oak, will bid it farewell. Africa awaits them.

In utter contrast to the white, noisy, festive life in the branches of the oak, is that other life which, strange, silent and somber, exists below the thickly growing fronds of bracken springing up in the shadow of the cork oaks. Of this I have some curious memories.

In poor autumns, when great stretches of the marsh are dry, the great carrion birds feast on the many animals which die from lack of food and water. A Black Vulture, a Griffin Vulture and Magpies join together to eat in a strange sort of unity.

By August of one rainy year the bracken was over my head, so that I walked in a strange, almost lightless forest, and so concealed, I was able to observe the nests in the cork oaks without the birds seeing me. I would stay there for hours, and when I tired of peering upwards through the foliage at the white madhouse, I would lie on the springy floor of last year's dry fronds and enter that other world, hidden below the bracken. Little by little the light grew stronger, as my eyes recovered from the glare of the outside world; here and there a ray of sunlight like a golden lance broke through among the prevailing colors of dull grey and faded green, and a cloudy vapor hung listlessly as if this were a miniature jungle. I was not alone in this deeply peaceful stillness: other life existed around me in the bracken.

The wild boar were often there in search of fallen heron nestlings; once I saw a lynx advancing warily through that shadowy jungle; and snakes,

The large and diverse geographical region that is Doñana is the reason for the incredible variety of flora and fauna. In the island-like nests of the Coot, and in the colorful Goldfinch which makes its home in the branches of an osier, we see small parts of this disparate world.

Some inhabitants of the large "aviaries" now situated in the old cork oaks on the edge of the marsh once clothed in white the great heathery area of La Algaida in Doñana. The Cattle Egrets, the majority of which now nest near La Rocina, together with the most important colony of White Herons in Europe formed the largest part of the birds populating the "aviaries" in the heather.

The splendid antlers of the bucks are the classic ornaments of the parched marsh in late summer.

some drawn by the coolness and others, in the evening, coming to hunt the toads at the edge of the marsh, were frequently to be seen slithering past.

One day, hearing the sounds of wild boar approaching, I got down on hands and knees like a quadruped, and in this absurd position I faced the direction of the sounds, with the wind blowing towards me. After a few minutes a sow and three young pigs appeared, to find themselves confronted by this strange creature. The five of us froze: they, with their inquiring snouts trying to catch my scent, and I, with my superior vision, observing them at my pleasure, without so much as blinking. We stayed

An outstanding view from the Cork Oak Wood.

The Buzzards habitually nest in isolated cork oaks, and although some pairs prefer to be near the marsh because of the various prey to be found there, the wide range of this predator's diet allows it to live in virtually any habitat.

The edge of the marsh, in the shelter of the cork oaks, is the preferred habitat of the Fallow Deer. There, their reproductive cycle takes place, except the actual birth, during which time they hide themselves in more thickly covered and protected areas.

Although this bird only carries a toad in its beak, the Black Kites are the greatest enemy of the heronries. One year, because of a bad drought and the consequent lack of food, the Herons abandoned their nests, and the Black Kites killed almost all of the helpless nestlings.

After several centuries this great cork oak, in which so many birds have been hatched and raised, is now twisted and deformed like a fairy tale giant. Little by little, it ends its long existence, strewing the ground with leafless branches covered in grey cork bark.

like this for some time —impossible to calculate how long —all of us motionless with surprise; and they would never know just how strange an encounter they had had that afternoon under the cork oaks of Caño de la Abulaga.

With the first days of autumn, and sometimes a little earlier, the edge of the cork oak wood becomes the scene of those matches of love and war which first the red and then the fallow deer dispute in the dry, brown marsh, with the gigantic cork oaks as immutable and solemn witnesses to the noisy bellowing and hoarse grunting.

Finally, as winter approaches, the cork oaks return to a more seemly natural gravity. These trees are like great strong bodies, immense and self-assured, which hide an intense, silent life in their depths —just tolerating the other lesser lives which, thousands of times over, are born, live and then die around them.

Sovereigns of Doñana

Doñana possesses two jewels of the zoological world: the lynx and the imperial eagle. Both merit special mention here, as they stand out among the various and numerous fauna of these lands. They are the most powerful and perhaps the most beautiful species that live in the Reserve, and are now rarely found outside of it. The lynx is the lord of the scrubland, the sovereign of his preserve of Doñana, and the imperial eagle rules the skies. No more flexible muscles or bolder claws are to be found on the ground, nor such powerful wings in the sky. Both species possess the most effective natural defenses and are therefore the supreme predators of Doñana, the undisputed rulers of extensive territories. One of these eagles soaring through the immense expanse of blue sky over Doñana on its harlequin wings demonstrates all the beauty possible in a bird of prey. Likewise, to witness the monarch of the scrub moving his graceful feline body through brilliant green vegetation and to see him spring, audacious and deadly, upon the back of a larger, strong deer, is to accept his indubitable sovereignty.

The future of the Lynx in Doñana is very bright, and as long as its habitat remains unaltered the survival of this species is assured. Scenes such as this, of a pair of Lynxes placidly sunning themselves on a winter morning, can now be seen in the Reserve.

The Lynx population of Doñana is by far the most numerous in Europe, where this species can be considered virtually extinct. The species is now found only on the Iberian Peninsula and in some parts of Eastern Europe.

The Lynx

Centuries ago the lynx lived in most wooded areas of a great part of southern Europe. The species then experienced an absolute regression, so that today the population found in Doñana is the most numerous known anywhere. As is true with some other species, its almost complete eradication throughout the continent was caused by unrestrained, hunting— a result of the theory which prevailed until recently, that it was necessary to eliminate the predators in order to protect the other fauna. To those who practiced it, this policy proved to be more disastrous than could have been imagined, for by eliminating the predator, the biological balance of the natural community was irreparably altered.

In Doñana the lynx is found from the northern limits (Coto del Rey, Hato Blanco, Hato Raton) to the mouth of the Guadalquivir, discriminating little between the various areas; for although it prefers the scrubland of the rock rose, it hunts and dwells in the lentisk thickets and savin clumps and even in the reedbeds and blackberry patches on the border of the marsh. It has even been known to enter the water to hunt. For the lynx in Doñana there are no forbidden territories; as supreme monarch of these lands it extends its territories to where it wishes, as kings of men did before it.

Although not excessively shy, the lynx is difficult to observe, owing mainly to its usual nocturnal habits. In the winter, however, on cold days or when heavy rain has left its coverts wet, it leaves the thick scrub to laze in the sun, or hunts in open territory at any hour of the day.

One morning early in January, I was leaving Doñana by the access road to the Palace. At ten o'clock,

As with all felines, the Lynx has beauty of form, elegance of movement, and extremely well-developed senses, especially those of sight and hearing. This king of the scrubland, which with an incredible leap catches a partridge in full flight, as easily as it kills an adult deer with a bite from its fangs, has its black legend, which we recount in the text.

as the car passed Km 2, I saw a pair of lynxes relaxing in the sunshine on the ridge of a dune. I stopped the car only about thirty meters from them, but they did no more than look. The splendid male, strong-legged and broad of back, with a luxuriant beard and thick, black whiskers, was every inch the patriarch beside his mate, who was slimmer and smaller-headed; the black-spotted, ocher skin of both animals was gilded by the sun. I stopped the engine and while Litia photographed them, I took some film shots in 16mm. A little later they indolently rose and disappeared from our view. Camera in hand, I got out of the car and followed them. As I had supposed, they had only walked off slowly into the rock rose scrub. On two other occasions, both in winter, I have observed lynxes basking in the sun —once at two o'clock in the afternoon— each time at a short distance, but without my presence causing a hurried retreat.

The hunting prowess of the Lynx is unquestioned. Its formidable weapons and agility make all the fauna of Doñana its potential prey, and eventually all come within its predatory range. The victims which fall to this undisputed sovereign range from the rabbit, which is its basic diet, to the large deer, which it occasionally kills.

In January the lynx comes in heat, and in April the litter is born. By early May the females are to be seen accompanied by two or three young. The lairs for breeding may be found in the hollow trunks of cork oaks, cavities under tangled thickets of vegetation, or old storks' nests high up in the trees. Juan Espinar Bernal told me he once found a lair with two kittens in the dense, flattened crown of a pine tree close to the beach, in the district of Las Marismillas; and José Boixo Sánchez (these two men both being Senior Guards at Doñana) discovered a lair in a clump of savin, some two and one-half meters above the ground.

Its excellent hunting abilities and natural defenses mean that the lynx has no basic problem of survival, as is shown by its increasing numbers in Doñana. Its basic diet is the rabbit, which it hunts by stalking. The following narration by another guard describes its technique:

"The light was beginning to fade, and I had stopped my horse to light a cigarette. As I was about to continue on I noticed something move in the scrub. Looking closely, I saw that it was a lynx, moving quickly and soundlessly, its shoulders hunched and its body flattened and stretched out, opening its way through the scrub

One morning, when the light was still dim, a female Lynx —stretching low and creeping through dry sedge with feline grace— stalked a band of geese. Then... a sudden burst of speed, a leap through the vegetation ending in a resounding impact, and a cloud of white feathers flying from the slashed breast of a wild goose. Later, the camera caught this scene of one of the young amusing itself with the last shreds of flesh.

like a snake. It took no notice of me; its gaze was fixed on a rabbit feeding at the edge of a small clearing. Without pausing in its advance it leaped on the rabbit - and, Madre mía, I've never seen anything like it! I saw later from its pug marks that it had jumped five paces."

There are many cases of lynxes hunting partridge and duck in flight, springing into the air and using their agile fore-paws and sharp claws to catch the bird. During spring of those years when flooding has made the rabbits scarce, the nesting ducks become the lynx's main prey. Adult red and fallow deer are hunted less frequently, since much more effort must be expended by the lynx; and then they normally hunt in pairs. Professor Valverde writes the following about the death of a doe and three fawns:

"At the height of the throat on either side the fangs had made seven punctures, from five to seven millimeters in diameter, piercing the skin cleanly. A quick dissection showed that the muscles below the skin had been completely destroyed. The glottis was partly torn out, and the hyoid on the right side was ripped. The carcasses of the fawns and of the adult doe all showed similar wounds."

The guards are unanimous in saying that the lynx is capable of killing an adult stag. Near Charco del Toro a large one was found dead, and from a study of the wounds and tracks it was clear that this was the work of a lone lynx.

The lynx of Doñana has its "black legend" —not surprising in a creature so lovely yet so powerful. It is accused of killing for the sake of killing, of eating much less than it kills, of a lust for blood. In this respect the Senior Guard of Las Marismillas told me, "The lynx kill many fallow deer fawns which they leave almost uneaten. One day in July, among the bullrushes at the edge of the marsh, in the district of Ribete de Pocito, I found seven fawns killed by lynxes."

Juan Domínguez, talking about past days, when the guards used to trap rabbits for their cooking pots (the nearest food supply center being the village of Almonte, some forty kil-

ometers distant), said that many times he had found rabbits caught in traps and partly eaten by a lynx. I would not dream of disputing the conclusive proofs held by the objective and sincere guards of Doñana, but it is my opinion that these habits are due to neither bloodthirstiness nor sadism, but simply to the insolent extravagance of these proud hunters.

The Imperial Eagle

Another species protected by the sanctuary of Doñana is the imperial eagle (águila heliaca). The few remaining pairs of the Spanish imperial eagle are scattered throughout some three-quarters of the Iberian Peninsula, but they are so rare that only in Doñana, where there is a more numerous population, is one likely to see them. However, what we have just called a "numerous population" consists of only twelve pairs. But twelve pairs of imperial eagles —the Koh-i-noor of birds— are a zoological treasure.

For thirteen years now the number of imperial eagles in Doñana has remained stable, and this stability has two fundamental causes: the increased longevity of this species, and the fact that it has reached saturation point in this isolated redoubt. There is nothing unusual about their longevity, since it is general among the big raptorial birds; and of these twelve pairs, two have reached the age of sterility. With respect to the saturation, it is

This Imperial Eagle, which can fill some great birds with such terror and panic that they commit suicide, is now simply a suffering mother, bearing the heat of the sun to shelter her nestling in the shade of her arched wings.

All the adult's care of their young is to no avail against the continuing diminishing of the species —one of the rarest and most beautiful in the world. Probably only a radical change in human attitudes towards wildlife will prevent the last Imperial Eagle from being displayed in a museum within fifty years.

not surprising if we remember that each pair of these great eagles needs an extremely large territory, which in Doñana covers an average of 5,000 hectares. It is fascinating to think that in the age of the skyscraper there should exist a creature so magnificent that it needs 5,000 hectares for its solitary dominion. The imperial eagles of Doñana are like feudal lords who maintained dominance over their vast estates in the Middle Ages. They lift their wings and soar in those clear, silent blue skies, while Man suffocates in smoke and noise.

As they are threatened with extinction, the few remaining examples of this bird are of great interest to ornithologists all over the world. It is estimated that this Spanish sub-species will have disappeared within fifty years. The reasons are obvious: an already extremely reduced population; a desperately low rate of reproduction (0.75 chicks per pair per year); and the

Twelve pairs comprise the total Imperial Eagle population in Doñana; and this small number constitutes the most numerous population anywhere in existence.

killing —apparently impossible to control— of young birds which leave the safety of the territories where they are raised. Only with a radical change in Man's attitude towards the preservation of nature, will it be possible for the Spanish imperial eagle to survive.

The imperial eagles build their enormous nests in the crowns of tall cork oaks or pines, each year choosing a new tree within their territory, where the female lays two or three eggs at the end of February or in early March. One or two of the eggs are usually infertile, and it is rare for more than one chick to survive, for various reasons, including cannibalism, which we will discuss later.

The following are extracts from notes on the behavioral norms of adults and nestlings, made from my own observations:

"7th May, 1970. Mancha del Marqués (in an observation blind). 15.30 hours: The same adult returns,

Each pair of Imperial Eagles in Doñana has its own territory of about five thousand hectares —an empire necessitated by its grand nature. To lose it would be, for this bird, like receiving a death warrant.

bearing in its talons a female mallard which it drops into the nest. Feeds the nestling with pieces of rabbit which it had brought earlier.

15.40 hours: Stays in the nest, its strong body shielding the chick from the high wind.

"17.10 hours: Moves branches from the right hand side of the nest to the front and back. Makes a hollow in the center of the nest, pushes the chick into this space and covers it with its body —the wind is very strong.

"10th May (same place. 09.45 hours: The rain becomes heavier. The adult settles in the nest and the chick quickly pushes under it, remaining completely covered. The rain runs off the adult's arched wings, making a puddle in the hollow of its back. A ceaseless trickle of water falls from its beak.

"13th May (same place). 16.10 hours: The nestling emerges from under the female's wings. She immediately begins to tear pieces from a rabbit and feeds them to it. Its crop swells quickly, and it will only accept very small pieces. This meal lasts for fifteen minutes, and the female shows ability in breaking up the prey, immediate comprehension when the chick rejects large pieces, lack of hurry and a gentleness which I have not seen before. At one stage the female

The reddish color of the chick's brilliant feathers differs greatly from the harlequin colors of the adult.

offers her young a kidney, which it rejects; she then pecks pieces from it until, with great patience, she has persuaded the nestling to eat as much as possible."

The imperial eagle, like the lynx, has no problems in obtaining food, for it is a powerful and able hunter. Except for the large mammals, all the inhabitants of Doñana are potential prey for this mighty bird. The imperial eagle's diet ranges from rabbit —its usual prey— through a wide spectrum of fauna, including hares, flamingos, geese, ducks, snakes, and even great bustards.

Since its territory covers such large areas it is seldom that man is able to watch it hunt. However, over many scores of years its methods of hunting have been occasionally observed by guards and naturalists, and the following passages are taken from their concise descriptions.

I have at my disposal many references to the imperial eagle's hunting of rabbits, but because of Abel Chapman's high standing as a naturalist, I prefer to use one from *Rough Notes on Ornithology*:

"A pair of Imperial Eagles are on a hunting flight, scrutinizing their territory. Suddenly one of them appears to see something, and pauses for a moment in flight, readying itself in a swift dive, making a clearly audible rushing sound. Then one hears a violent blow on the earth. A couple of seconds later the eagle rises again in flight, emitting harsh cries, with a rabbit in its talons."

The hunting of hares by this eagle was watched on two occasions by Curro Chico, the guard of the El Puntal district. When described in his clear, precise idiom it acquires the wings of victory, the muteness of tragedy: "I was riding along a track of firm ground when suddenly a hare broke from cover in front of me. The

The Imperial Eagle remains in the air for many hours, covering its enormous hunting territory.

eagle, flying very high, saw it and with its wings closed, dropped like a stone with a humming noise that made my hair stand on end. It caught the hare and carried it off towards the scrubland."

On another occasion Curro Chico tells of a hare in Corral Quemado which sprang out from the edge of the pinewood and went racing across the dunes: "It could not have made a better target against the white sands. The eagle appeared suddenly and fell on the hare, spitting it on its sharp talons in full career without ever touching the ground."

Antonio Clarita, the grand patriarch of the marsh, has a great store of knowledge about the marsh birds, and his powers of observation are equal to those of any specialist. He once told Professor Valverde how the imperial eagle hunts geese, and since there is little variation from the version he recounted to me, I quote the passage as Valverde wrote it in a scientific publication:

"Each winter a pair of eagles from Las Marismillas comes to hunt in Las Nuevas, a little after sunrise. Their favorite prey is the goose; they never attack ducks. Sometimes they hunt singly, but more often as a team.

"If there is only one eagle, flying high, and the geese do not see it, it drops vertically on its prey and the goose, in the panic of surprise, stupidly allows itself to be killed on the ground. The noise of the collision between the two birds can be heard from a long way off.

"But more often the gaggle takes flight as the eagle swoops. The eagle then half opens its wings and changes direction, perhaps catching a goose as it rises from the water. With its bunched talons held forward it deals the goose a tremendous blow in the breast, and they both fall to the ground, where the eagle eats its victim, never carrying it away.

"However, it more frequently fails, and then it begins a tireless pursuit of the gaggle —which sometimes lasts over an hour— attempting to separate one goose from its fellows. Time after time it hurls itself against the gaggle, and at each attack the gaggle closes up and eludes its tormentor. It is sel-

The Imperial Eagle's hunting capacities ensure an adequate diet for its young. From its usual prey, which is the rabbit, to the heavy bustard, it is an exceptional species which does not come within the range of the Imperial Eagle's talons in Doñana.

Fanning the air with its great wings, the prey dangling from its talons, the Imperial Eagle approaches its nest, —a magnificent scene.

dom that the eagle is able to cut out one bird, but if this happens the goose is lost. It tries to reach the water, and if it is successful it escapes, even though the water is shallow. But often, if the goose dives the eagle follows and catches it.

"Usually the pair hunt together, and they rarely fail." (Here follows a detailed description of the team's tactics).

"The geese have such a fear of the eagle that when they catch sight of one they rise immediately from the water and flee rapidly, swerving in evasive action as they go. When one sees geese behaving in this fashion, one knows that an eagle will soon appear."

We could continue to describe the techniques used by the imperial eagle in hunting various types of prey. We could speak at length of the suicidal behavior of the flamingos. When one of these birds sees an eagle approach, it becomes so panic-stricken that it closes its wings and falls to the earth, killing itself. Again, we could describe the pathetic sight of a suddenly mute colony of spoonbills, with an imperial eagle perched in the middle of it, selecting its prey, while the possible victims simply await their doom. But we shall end with a description of the imperial eagle's hunting of the great bustard, one of the largest flying birds. Verner gives a beautiful and precise account of this hunt in his work *My Life Among the Wild Birds of Spain:*

"One of the most memorable sights I ever witnessed was when I was among the Bustards in the spring of 1878. We were posted for a drive, and the great birds, as so often happens, refused to be driven and elected to swing in their flight, and passed clear of our line of guns. At this moment a White Shouldered Eagle (Aquila Adalberti) which had been sailing in great circles high over the plain, suddenly descended and with a falcon-like swoop struck one of the Bustards in the flock, knocking out a cloud of feathers."

We always try to catalogue powerful animals as either potential winners or losers when in competition with other powerful animals. There is bound to be some reader, therefore, who will ask himself who would be the victor in an imaginary contest between these two monarchs of Doñana. There is only one known result of what was probably a duel. On the morning of the 27th of December, 1969, the guard Antonio Otero discovered a dead Lynx on the banks of the Lake of Santa Olalla. It was a young animal, born that same year. At the Palace its body was dissected and examined, and there remained no doubt: the talons that had pierced the throat of the young lynx could only have belonged to an imperial eagle. This, of course, is not evidence of the eagle's supremacy, for perhaps with a fully-grown lynx the result would be different.

e majestic Imperial Eagle —king of the skies in Doñ-
a.

Marshes

In June, 1962, the World Council of Ornithologists met in New York. The following is taken from the minutes of this meeting: "... the marshes of the Guadalquivir constitute the last sure refuge in Europe of the pink flamingo and some species of heron; ... it is an area where such rare and beautiful species breed as the white-headed duck, crested coot, purple gallinule and many others impossible to enumerate..."

It is not surprising that the marshes of the Lower Guadalquivir should have been the subject of international discussion at that time. As long ago as 1910 Abel Chapman, hunter and naturalist, had told the world of the grandeur of Doñanas fauna and described these unique untouched lands in his works *Wild Spain* and *Unexplored Spain*. The zoological wealth of this lost corner of Europe was further substantiated in 1957 by Julian Huxley. But only the man who has actually seen the marsh, fully or in part, can understand that without what appears to be exaggeration or

Before its waters recede and glades emerge, the marsh is a sea of indistinct horizons. At this moment the marsh forms what is possibly the largest lake in western Europe.

The Grey Lag Goose, which nests mainly in Scandinavia and Iceland, winters in great numbers on the marshes of the Guadalquivir. The many pools in the districts of Hinojos and Las Nuevas provide an ideal habitat for these northern emigrants. It is these wild geese which so strongly characterize the marsh in winter. When the great gaggles rise in the air, they form such huge masses that they hide the sun and shadow the waters.

This is a frequent sight in the skies over the lakes of Doñana.

superfluous adjectives, it is not possible to describe adequately these indivisible lands and waters.

I was riding one of those sure-footed marsh horses which learn to swim as foals. The horizon of the Mari López district, illuminated by the rising sun, seemed to be mantled in snow and the surfaces of the pools were as if white-washed. Only occasional flashes of gold indicated patches of water. A string of some fifty great crested grebe flying low overhead created a brief disparate note of grey in an otherwise dazzling white scene. Suddenly, the report of a gun was heard, disturbing the silence of the marsh. The white covering on the water seemed to rise several meters and hang suspended for a moment; then, swelling strangely, it filled all the space within view. There were eighty thousand birds flying overhead! Not even the eyes which watched the spectacle that May morning from among the reeds of the pools of Mari López could comprehend the true meaning of beauty in the marshes.

Man is strange to the marsh, and the men of the marsh are unusual as well. Their huts of dry, interwoven straw, exactly the same as those which were used in the Later Middle Ages, are found scattered throughout these remote regions. Within: a world which we no longer recognize. Without: the land of the children of generations lost in time; the land which they love for its beauty and, above all, because it was their cradle.

Perhaps the uniqueness of the marsh can be attributed to two fundamental factors: its virginity, and the profound changes which it undergoes during the course of the year. Miraculously, all of the immense region has been virtually unchanged, and some 40,000 hectares remain in the same primitive condition in which they were during the Middle Ages. With respect to its seasonal variations, we can be sure that anyone who has seen the marsh in winter, when only the transitory islets called "vetas" emerge from the flood, would not recognize it in summer when, except for the mudholes and an occasional pool, it has become a desert-like wilderness of cracked earth.

The annual cycle of the marshes begins with the autumn rains. The baked, dusty soil is transformed into an endless quagmire. The dry, fallen stems of sedge rot in the mud; the wild geese return from summer quarters in Scandinavia, and thousands of ducks of many species begin to arrive and occupy the most flooded areas. The seeds of sedge and grasswort provide food for these northern visitors which, together with the non-migratory species, by the end of the year constitute one of the greatest populations of aquatic brirds in the world.

It is not a rarity to see the sun clouded over by flocks of birds in flight. If a count were made of the frequency of this occurrence, the figures would seem to be absurdly high.

The advent of February brings little change to the scene. The earth remains flooded and the endless sea of still water continues to shelter thousands of birds.

It was perhaps at this point that the "patero," the time-honored duck

The saline mudflats are the area which supports least life in Doñana. During the last century, the Camel was introduced to and thrived in this desert-like region.

hunter, without whom no portrait of the marsh is complete, made his appearance in the sleepy waters of the lagoons —waters that seemed to be as wide as the sea and were covered with wild duck. In the winter the patero, who was practicing this science before it was ever learned by others, would spend seven days on the marsh and one in his hut, to deposit game and to collect fresh gunpowder. But he is now a figure of the past.

He carried (I use the past tense, because the man I am endeavoring to portray is now nonexistent) an enormous, clumsy fowling piece, consisting of a stout stock and a cylindrical muzzle four or five centimeters in diameter. The length of the weapon was about 1.60 meters. These shotguns were fashioned in Seville by artisan armorers, and were notorious for the variation of their characteristics. In 1930, one of these guns would have cost approximately twenty-five "duros" (at today's value a few dollars). Its charge of black powder and four or five caliber shot, was five times greater than that used in normal shotguns of the largest caliber (12 gauge, which they contemptuously called "little shotgun"). The "duck shotgun" or "big shotgun" could kill up to thirty-five brace of teal with one shot. It is a curious fact that thirty-five brace of teal represented, in the peculiar manner of counting used by the pateros, one hundred and forty birds because, for them, the basic unit

In the salt water of these lagoons lives a small crustacean which is eaten by the Flamingos and provides the substance that gives their feathers a lovely pink color.

The long, widely-spaced horns, their ends turning upwards; the reddish hide —copper-colored in the sun— and the lean body, make the marsh cattle a singular breed, well-suited to their unusual habitat. Completely wild, these cattle serve no purpose and are hunted as game.

The agile Fallow Deer, with their graceful movements, prefer the clear open territory of the marsh to the harsh closed-in scrubland.

was the mallard, and they established the equivalent for other species according to size. Thus, a brace of widgeon was three widgeon, a brace of teal was four teal, etc.

If we had to mention two outstanding characteristics of the duck hunter, these would have to be his skill and his valor. His skill included a profound knowledge of the psychology of the wild duck, which enabled him to approach a "concha" (1) while hiding behind his bridleless horse which appeared to be grazing. Advancing in a zig-zag, with the wind in his favor, he was able to get as close as twenty or twenty-five paces from the birds which, meanwhile, had been banding closer and closer together, as is their habit when puzzled or uneasy —the effect that this clever maneuver had on them. This was because the horse was not behaving as other horses— there was something in its actions that, while not sufficient to startle them, left them suspicious and doubtful.

Courage and endurance were also attributed to the patero, who day after day bore the cold loneliness of the marshes in winter; courage also, to fire the shot which, as his scarred face and limbs showed, did not always scatter its deadly load from the mouth of the barrel.

If only for this, we should like to give "El Quico Llano", from Coria del Río; "Telégrafos" of Lebrija; "Quinta";

---

(1) *Local name for a flock of ducks, numerous and closely gathered on water.*

In spring, when the marsh has become Europe's gigantic breeding ground, the birdlife is hidden under a thick tangle of vegetation. In silence, the great mass of living protein grows and grows.

"El Manco" and all the others lost in the darkness of time, the mention they deserve as virtuosos of the "big shotgun."

At the end of February begins the massive exodus of the northern migratory birds, back towards the distant tundra of Lapland, where once again Nature will impose her unalterable law of reproduction.

In March the appearance of the marsh changes daily. The temperature becomes milder and the layer of water begins slowly to disappear, covered by a thick green carpet of galingale and other sedge. To punt across the marsh at this time of year in a "cajón" —a small, flat-bottomed skiff— or to be towed through the water by a horse, is an unforgettable experience. The cajon, cutting its way through the luxuriant vegetation, which surrenders itself gently to this slow advance, carries us for hours on a journey which we could wish eternal, over an endless, clear backwater, where the nests of coots, little grebes and black terns, of great crested grebes and purple herons, obstruct our passage like diminutive, green floating islands. And how pleasant it is, by simply stretching out ones arm, to be able to pick up those warm eggs: white, grey or mottled; to hear the wings of birds fanning the air about us; and to feel at one, in the absolute solitude of the marsh, with all the strange, multiform life surrounding us.

And when, at the slow rhythmical pace of the horse in water up to its girth, we find ourselves gliding

In all this world of birds, where the palette of the painter would empty itself of colors, the simple little Reed Warblers, which owe their name to the reedbeds where they live and hang their nests, might be overlooked, like so many others which we have left behind, their trilling lost in the immenseness of the marsh.

through a sea of emerald sedge, our pulses slow, the soft murmur of the rippling water gives us a lazy indolence, and the senses are lulled sweetly to sleep, only to awaken and drink in this very special beauty. Things begin to take on strange dimensions, outside the normal order of our lives... and perhaps we wish for an everlasting dream within them, with our hands trailing pleasurably through the unmoving waters, the lucern and sedge brushing our faces with the soft, pliant sway of their cool fronds.

Coots abound, and their nests of roughly-woven reeds are so numerous that in the time of the professional egg collector the quantity of eggs gathered in spring was as high as perhaps two thousand per day. Taking into account the fact that these collectors —children of the marsh— gathered only fresh eggs, and that they were unable to reach more than a small fraction of the nests, it is easy to imagine the tremendous number of eggs that the huge coot population produces.

Towards the end of April the galingale and other sedges which form the basic vegetation of the great, flooded jungle, have grown to such an extent that they are virtually impenetrable. It is now impossible to cross the marsh by boat. The green tangle is passable only on a tough, experienced horse.

Everything exudes life and plenty. A well-known European ecologist has

"Skywatcher" is the regional name given to the Little Bittern found throughout the lower Guadalquivir. The simple eloquence of the rustic tongue has succeeded in capturing the essence of this bird, which when alone adopts a hieratic posture, lifting its head to the sky. It lives and nests in the densest of the tall reedbeds.

Comprising in Doñana the most important population of its species in Europe, the "noveleta", by which curious regional name the Black-necked Grebe is known, calls in its cooing voice and in a variety of harmonious cries from the dense reedgrass. Its jet black neck and fan of golden feathers appear behind little ruby-like eyes. In the pools of Las Nuevas these beautiful grebes have formed colonies of as many as two thousand birds.

The Purple Gallinule is known as the Blue Cock locally. The carmine colored beak, which extends upward to form a horny covering over the forehead, and the bright indigo color of its feathers present a delightful contrast to the white crowfoot blossoms which surround it.

stated that the quantity of protein produced in the marshlands of the Guadalquivir by the reproduction of birdlife, is far greater than that which would be yielded by any type of livestock in an area of the same size and with the richest pastures. The sedge bears its ocher flowers and spills yellow pollen over the dense green carpet. Purple herons —glowing coals of fire in the sunlight— emerge from the green abundance; gadwalls and mallards can be seen easily, followed by their ducklings —an enchanting retinue which file behind their mother as she looks for a hiding place for them in the copious vegetation. In the populous colonies of coot can be seen both the old nests —only a bare platform remaining to recall the previous annual gathering—

The Purple Gallinule is one of the strangest-looking inhabitants of the marsh. It is a bird of archaic structure and is therefore of great ornithological value. It nests in the most hidden corners of the marsh, and also in the bullrushes of Lake Dulce. Its nestlings, at birth, seem to have come from different stock. What will one day be waxy blue feathers is now thick black plumage, and in place of this pearly little beak will grow another —large strong and red.

and the others full of life, with the nestlings struggling to force their scarlet heads from the broken shells. It is at the same time a lively fete with hundreds of young birds swarming in this flooded forest, diving, swimming, attempting to fly, and mingling their piping cries with the serious calls of their progenitors.

If during the spring, when life is so splendidly scattered throughout Doñana, the huge population remains hidden and quiet beneath the thick covering of vegetation, in contrast, during autumn and winter the skies —pale indigo, grey, or covered with dark clouds— are filled with graceful, vigorous wings. The Black-tailed Godwit, in bands of thousands, are the performers in this aerial display.

To watch the gentle Black-winged Stilt as it approaches its nest is to enjoy one of those exquisite little scenes which are usually missed in grandiose settings. It is a ballet of suspicion. Gentle movements, now bold, now timid, bring it gradually closer. It brushes its feathers against the small grassworts, curves its flight around the large ones, and opens the vegetation with its dancing body. Then, on the nest, placing its legs on either side of the eggs and folding its wings, it lowers itself weightlessly, carefully, onto the unhatched nestlings.

In this wild land, men like this, their age unknown and their origin forgotten in time, are faithful witnesses of the unrecorded past. They pass the verbal history to their sons as they themselves received it from their fathers. Only in this way can we explain the fact that customs and memories eight centuries old survive and form part of the lives of some marsh families.

Without any protection, in a slight hollow in the ground, the Pratincole lays its brownish eggs. This rudimentary nest is often found on dry cowpats, which insulate the eggs from the heat. When the eggs hatch, hundreds of young birds are dispersed about the dry earth. However, their camouflage and their ability to remain absolutely still can make them almost invisible, even in the most open territory.

At intervals a colony of black terns attracts our attention with shrill cries. These colonies, and those of the gull-billed tern, are curious examples of social behavior. The nests are closely grouped, and the birds defend their colony en masse, preventing the close approach of any animal, including Man. This defense system is so effective that other, less socially-developed species with a lesser ability to defend themselves, build their nests within the shelter of these bellicose tribes.

The order of defense is different between the black terns and the gull-billed terns. In both cases, when an intruder approaches, the great mass of

The predator most common in the marsh is the Marsh Harrier. With its wings slightly raised in a vee, and with its low, zig-zag flight, its unmistakable form is seen flying over many kilometers. Its hunting capacity is poor, however, and in the spring it preys on the nestlings of aquatic birds, with which it feeds its young.

Pink Flamingos blanket the Lucio del Membrillo. There the birds color the shallow water of this beautiful lagoon, which is surrounded by high banks of white sand. On some days, as many as six thousand flamingos can be seen in this idyllic setting.

No bigger than a Turtle Dove, the Whiskered Terns form tight-knit colonies to defend themselves from predators. Their defense system is so effective that other birds nest close to these colonies in order to benefit from the protection that these well-organized sea swallows give them. Even the most powerful raptors will not enter the territory of these birds which en masse, with a deafening war cry, hurl themselves against anything which comes too near — including Man.

The brave, agile Whiskered Tern, which will even defy an Imperial Eagle in defense of its colony.

The Little Grebe is the smallest of the marsh grebes. Its nest, a tiny floating island anchored to the vegetation, forms a green pedestal for its serene image.

Habituation to the presence of humans is common in many birds and animals, and the restless Redshank is no exception. During the incubation period within the leafy shelter of a veta, the woody cover of the grass-wort, or the bareness of a little hollow in the ground, the bird's lack of alarm allows a very close approach.

When the sun of late spring is drying up the waters; when the arid mudflats are becoming dusty plains, when this desert-like region seems to be devoid of any form of life, the Pin-tailed Sand Grouse is splendid in gay contrast — lovely grey feathers speckled with lemon yellow, chestnut-colored wings orange-tinged face of the male, black bands crossing his chest. When it beats its pointed wings, it fills the warm air of the marsh with a loud croaking noise.

the greater part of the annual floods. These vetas appear as small islands scattered throughout the marshes, occasionally linked to form a relatively long chain. Over the higher areas grows an abundant and compact vegetation consisting mainly of thistles, ideal material for the nests of web-footed birds and certain waders.

The arrival of May is saluted in the marshes with a myriad of broken shells and new life scattered all over its now shrunken waters. The motley crowd of young web-footed and wading birds is ruthlessly decimated by raptors, herons and rodents. The nests are continually beseiged by all the predators. A great part of this infant flesh feeds other young mouths, thanks to the parents who, naturally, follow their instincts.

During the entire month this cold, confused struggle for survival takes place all over the marsh. Some eat and others are eaten, but the great mass of living protein continues to grow.

By June the water has almost disappeared; the green plants turn brown and the withered sedge lies fallen on

In this manner, following immemorial custom, one crosses the shallow water. The cajon, a small flat-bottomed skiff is fastened to the tail of a muscular marsh horse. Behind this strong animal, the boat slices through the forest of emerald sedge.

The Great Crested Grebe, when it leaves its nest, covers it with vegetation to protect the eggs from temperature variations as well as reduce their visibility from the air.

the dry, cracked mud. The generating force of the life-giving marsh is finished, its fertile womb exhausted after so many births; and the young leave the great mother in search of a new life on the interior lakes of Doñana and the winding reaches of the Guadalquivir.

The wide, beautiful lagoons, clear and still, no longer exist. As each day passes, the water level falls lower, transforming green-festooned waters into hot quagmires, where carp now die in countless numbers. Their corpses which in some places lie in evil-

In August, the limit of thirst and death is reached in the marsh. The carcasses of dead animals rot in the sun, and their entrails fill the bellies of the Vultures and Buzzards — the marsh's emblems in the summer.

After May, the water level decreases daily until the water that remains is warm and muddy. The carp, which recently swam in still, clear water, now lie rotting in countless numbers on the hot mire.

smelling mounds, are food for herons and black kites.

So we come to July. The general exodus is completed. The marsh is now a lifeless steppe, an arid, burnt-out land. Its inhabitants of the previous months have migrated, and those that remain die under the fiery sun which bakes this naked world.

The Pool of Geese is the sole watery refuge in these 40,000 hectares of desert-like plain, where the only shade is that cast by the bodies of those who visit it and where there is no water other than that which remains in the water bottles.

August marks the limit of death and draught in the marsh. The last pools dry up, and where before life cried out so strongly and splendidly, nothing now remains but a nitrous surface of scored brown clay, dried-out and warped like a ghastly mosaic. In the Chujarro mudhole the last carp flap in the mire; the land finally loses almost all sign of life. The hides of dead cattle blacken in the sun and their intestines are food for the vultures —those terrible representatives of life in the marsh in summer.

Only a straying hedgehog and a few rodents remain, the last vestiges of life in these lands which in spring formed one of the greatest breeding grounds in Europe. The marsh is a colossus which does not permit half-measures. Life and death succeed each other inexorably, without mitigation.

The marsh at the end of the summer. The cracked earth extends endlessly. The barren earth is like a mosaic of death. Only short months before, the greatest concentration of aquatic birds in the world lived and bred on the water that covered this desert of mud.

If we had claimed through words and pictures to have captured on paper the essence of Doñana, we would by now have recognized our failure; for Doñana cannot adequately be described in even the most ambitious of books. Doñana is more than heather and gorse, the lynx's leap, the flight of the imperial eagle, or the thunderous love-calls of the deer... more than wing-filled skies and marshes with endless horizons.

Doñana remains immovable and untranslatable. It is like a huge museum in which each display case is a world of freedom, a world of natural, spontaneous beauty. There, values seem to be reversed, and proud Man feels diminished and overwhelmed by a quality he cannot comprehend.

You who may one day tread these lands, go prepared, for from them emanates life's most terrible drug—enslavement to the sublime.

List of the Zoological Species of Doñana

The following is a list of the zoological species which are native to Doñana and those which habitually visit there. Species which have been seen there only on rare occasions have been excluded.

Where the behavioral patterns differ in the population of one species, this will be indicated by the heading under which it is listed. In this way, it is possible to give a closer approximation of their representivity in Doñana.

The species marked with an asterisk are those which breed in Doñana.

English	Scientific name	Summer Visitors	Winter Visitors	Resident	Rare
FISH					
Eel	Anguilla anguilla			+	
Carp*	Cyprinus carpio			+	
Crucian carp*	Carassius carassius				
Gambusia*	Gambusia affinis			+	
AMPHIBIANS				+	
Pleurodele*	Pleurodeles waltl				
Marbled Newt*	Triturus marmoratus				
Spanish Spade-foot Toad*	Pelobates cultripes			+	
Common Toad*	Bufo bufo			+	
Natterjack*	Bufo calamita			+	
Tree Frog*	Hyla arborea			+	
Common Frog*	Rana ridibunda			+	
REPTILES				+	
Spanish Terrapin*	Clemmys caspica			+	
European Pond Tortoise*	Emys orbicularis			+	
Iberian Land Tortoise*	Testudo graeca			+	
Wall Gecko*	Tarentola mauritanica			+	
Blind Lizard*	Blanus cinereus			+	
Eyed Lizard*	Lacerta lepida			+	
Common Lizard*	Lacerta hispanica				
Algerian Sand Racer*	Psammodromus algirus			+	
Fringe-fingered Lizard*	Acanthodactylus erythrurus			+	
Round-bodied Skink*	Chalcides bedriagai			+	
Striped Skink*	Chalcides striatus				
Ladder Snake*	Elaphe scalaris			+	
Southern Smooth Snake*	Coronella girondica			+	
Water Snake*	Natrix maura			+	
Ringed Snake*	Natrix natrix			+	
Montpellier Snake*	Malpolon monspessulanus				
Latastes Viper*	Vipera latasti			+	
BIRDS					
Great Crested Grebe*	Podiceps cristatus			+	
Black-necked Grebe*	Podiceps nigricollis			+	
Little Grebe*	Podiceps ruficollis			+	
Grey Heron*	Ardea cinerea	+			
Purple Heron*	Ardea purpurea	+			
Squacco Heron*	Ardeola ralloides	+			
Cattle Egret*	Ardeola ibis			+	
Little Egret*	Egretta garzetta	+		+	
Night Heron*	Nycticorax nycticorax	+			
Little Bittern*	Ixobrichus minutus	+			
Bittern*	Botaurus stellaris			+	
Glossy Ibis	Plegadis falcinellus		+		+
Spoonbill*	Platalea leucorodia	+			
White Stork*	Ciconia ciconia	+			
Creater Flamingo	Phoenicopterus ruber	+	+	+	
Grey Lag Goose	Anser anser		+		
Mallard*	Anas platyrhynchos		+	+	
Gadwall*	Anas strepera		+	+	
Pintail	Anas acuta		+		
Wigeon	Anas penelope		+		
Teal	Anas crecca		+		
Garganey	Anas querquedula		+		
Marbled Teal*	Anas angustirostris		+		

English	Scientific name	Summer Visitors	Winter Visitors	Resident	Rare
Shoveler	Anas clypeata		+		
Shelduck	Tadorna tadorna		+		
Ruddy Shelduck	Tadorna ferruginea		+	+	+
Red-crested Pochard*	Netta rufina	+	+		
Tufted Duck	Aythya fuligula		+		
Pochard*	Aythya ferina	+	+		
Ferruginous Duck*	Aythya nyroca	+	+		
White-headed Duck	Oxyura leucocephala			+	
Egyptian Vulture	Neophron percnopterus	+			
Griffon Vulture	Gyps fulvus	+	+		
Black Vulture	Aegypius monachus	+	+		
Imperial Eagle*	Aquila heliaca			+	
Bonelli's Eagle	Hieraaëtus fasciatus			+	
Booted Eagle*	Hieraaëtus pennatus	+			
Short-Toed Eagle*	Circaëtus gallicus	+			
Buzzard*	Buteo buteo			+	
Red Kite*	Milvus milvus		+	+	
Black Kite*	Milvus migrans	+			
Marsh Harrier*	Circus aeruginosus			+	
Hen Harrier	Circus cyaneus		+		+
Montagus Harrier*	Circus pygargus	+			
Peregrine	Falco peregrinus			+	
Hobby*	Falco subbuteo	+			
Lanner	Falco biarmicus				+
Merlin	Falco columbarius				+
Lesser kestrel*	Falco naumanni	+		+	
Kestrel*	Falco tinnunculus			+	
Red-legged Partridge*	Alectoris rufa			+	
Quail*	Coturnix coturnix			+	
Andalusian Hemipode*	Turnix sylvatica				+
Crane	Grus grus			+	
Great Bustard	Otis tarda	+	+		
Little Bustard	Otis tetrax	+	+		
Water Rail*	Rallus aquaticus			+	
Spotted Crake	Porzana porzana	+			
Baillon's Crake*	Porzana pusilla	+			
Corncrake	Crex crex	+			+
Purple Gallinule*	Porphyrio porphyrio			+	
Moorhen*	Gallinula chloropus			+	
Coot*	Fulica atra			+	
Crested Coot*	Fulica cristata			+	
Lapwing*	Vanellus vanellus		+	+	
Ringed Plover	Charadrius hiaticula		+		+
Little Ringed Plover	Charadrius dubius	+		+	
Kentish Plover	Charadrius alexandrinus				
Grey Plover	Pluvialis squatarola	+			
Golden Plover	Pluvialis apricaria	+			
Turnstone	Arenaria interpres	+			
Snipe	Gallinago gallinago	+			
Jack Snipe	Lymnocryptes minimus	+			
Curlew	Numenius arquata	+			
Whimbrel	Numenius phaeopus	+			
Black-tailed Godwit	Limosa limosa	+			
Black-tailed Godwit	Limosa lapponica	+			+
Common Sandpiper	Tringa hypoleucos	+			
Green	Tringa ochropus	+			
Redshank*	Tringa totanus	+	+	+	
Spotted Redshank	Tringa erythropus	+			
Greenshank	Tringa nebularia	+			
Ruff	Philomachus pugnax	+			
Knot	Calidris canutus	+			
Dunlin	Calidris alpina	+			
Curlew Sandpiper	Calidris ferruginea	+			
Sanderling	Calidris alba	+			
Avocet*	Recurvirostra avosetta	+		+	
Black-winged Stilt*	Himantopus himantopus	+		+	
Stone Curlew*	Burhinus oedicnemus			+	
Pratincole*	Glareola pratincola	+			
Lesser Black-back Gull	Larus fuscus		+		
Herring Gull	Larus argentatus		+	+	
Slender-billed Gull	Larus genei				+
Black-headed Gull	Larus ridibundus		+		
Black Tern*	Chlidonias niger	+			
Whiskered Tern*	Chlidonias hybrida	+			
Gull-billed Tern*	Gelochelidon nilotica	+			
Common Tern	Sterna hirundo	+			
Little Tern*	Sterna albifrons	+			
Black-bellied Sandgrouse*	Pterocles orientalis			+	+
Pin-tailed Sandgrouse*	Pterocles alchata			+	
Wood Pigeon*	Columba palumbus			+	
Turtle Dove*	Streptopelia turtur	+			
Cuckoo*	Cuculus canorus	+			+
Great Spotted Cuckoo*	Clamator glandarius	+			
Scops Owl*	Otus scops	+			+
Little Owl*	Athene noctua			+	
Long-eared Owl	Asio otus			+	+
Tawny Owl*	Strix aluco			+	
Barn Owl*	Tyto alba			+	
Red-necked Nightjar*	Caprimulgus ruficollis	+			
Swift	Apus apus	+			
Pallid Swift	Apus pallidus	+			
Alpine Swift	Apus melba	+			+
Kingfisher*	Alcedo atthis			+	+
Bee-eater*	Merops apiaster	+			
Roller*	Coracias garrulus	+			
Hoopoe*	Upupa epops	+			
Green Woodpecker⁻	Picus viridis			+	
Great Spotted Woodpecker⁺	Dendrocopos Major				

English	Scientific name	Summer Visitors	Winter Visitors	Resident	Rare
Wryneck	Jynx torquilla		+		+
Short-toed Lark*	Calandrella cinerea	+			
Lesser Short-toed Lark*	Calandrella rufescens	+		+	
Calandra Lark*	Melanocorypha calandra			+	
Crested Lark*	Galerida cristata			+	
Thekla Lark*	Galerida theklae			+	+
Sky Lark	Alauda arvensis			+	+
Wood Lark	Lullula arborea			+	
Swallow*	Hirundo rustica	+			
Meadow Pipit	Anthus pratensis		+		
Tawny Pipit*	Anthus campestris	+			
Spanish Yellow Wagtail*	Motacilla flava	+			
White Wagtail*	Motacilla alba		+	+	
Woodchat Shrike*	Lanius senator	+			
Great Grey Shrike*	Lanius excubitor			+	
Golden Oriole*	Oriolus oriolus	+			
Spotless Starling*	Sturnus unicolor			+	
Azure winged Magpie*	Cyanopica cyanus			+	
Magpie*	Pica pica			+	
Jackdaw*	Corvus monedula			+	
Raven*	Corvus corax			+	
Cetti's Warbler*	Cettia cetti			+	
Savi's Warbler*	Locustella luscinioides	+			
Fan-tailed Warbler*	Cisticola juncidis			+	
Reed Warbler*	Acrocephalus scirpaceus	+			
Great Reed Warbler*	Acrocephalus arundinaceus	+			
Melodious Warbler*	Hippolais polyglotta	+			
Orphean Warbler*	Sylvia hortensis	+			
Garden Warbler	Sylvia borin		+		
Whitethroat*	Sylvia communis	+			
Sardinian Warbler*	Sylvia melenocephala			+	
Spectacled Warbler*	Sylvia conspicillata	+			
Dartford Warbler*	Sylvia undata			+	
Rufous Bush Chat*	Cercotrichas galactotes	+			
Willow Warbler	Phylloscopus trochilus		+		
Chiffchaff	Phylloscopus collybita		+		
Spotted Flycatcher	Muscicapa striata	+			
Wheatear	Oenanthe oenanthe	+			
Black-eared Wheatear	Oenanthe hispanica	+			
Stonechat*	Saxicola torquata			+	
Robin*	Erithacus rubecula		+	+	
Blackbird*	Turdus merula			+	
Redwing	Turdus iliacus		+		
Song Thrush	Turdus philomelos		+		
Mistle Thrush	Turdus viscivorus	+	+		
Fieldfare	Turdus pilaris		+		+
Blue Tit*	Parus caeruleus			+	
Coal Tit	Parus ater	+	+		+
Great Tit*	Parus major			+	
House Sparrow*	Passer domesticus			+	
Spanish Sparrow*	Passer hispanoliensis	+		+	+
Tree Sparrow*	Passer montanus			+	+
Chaffinch	Fringilla coelebs	+	+		
Serin*	Serinus serinus	+	+	+	
Greenfinch	Carduelis chloris			+	
Goldfinch*	Carduelis carduelis			+	
Linnet	Acanthis cannabina	+	+	+	
Corn Bunting	Emberiza calandra			+	

MAMMALS

English	Scientific name	Summer Visitors	Winter Visitors	Resident	Rare
Hedgehog*	Erinaceus europaeus			+	
Savi's Pygmy Shrew*	Suncus etruscus			+	
White-toothed Shrew*	Crocidura russula			+	
Greater Horseshoe Bat	Rhinolophus ferrum-equinum			+	
Lesser Mouse-eared Bat	Myotis oxygnathus	+	+	+	
Schreiber's Bat	Miniopterus schreibersi	+	+		
Pipistrelle*	Pipistrellus pipistrellus			+	
Serotine	Vespertilio serotinus			+	
Rabbit*	Oryctolagus cuniculus			+	
Brown Hare*	Lepus capensis			+	
Garden Dormouse*	Eliomys quercinus			+	
Water Vole*	Arvicola sapidus			+	
Mediterranean Pine Vole*	Pitymys duodecimcostatus			+	
Woodmouse*	Apodemus sylvaticus			+	
Black Rat*	Rattus rattus			+	
Brown Rat*	Rattus norvegicus			+	
House Mouse*	Mus musculus			+	
Fox*	Vulpes vulpes			+	
Badger*	Meles meles			+	
Weasel*	Mustela nivalis			+	+
Polecat*	Putorius putorius			+	+
Otter*	Lutra lutra			+	+
Mongoose*	Herpestes ichneumon			+	
Genet*	Genetta genetta			+	+
Wildcat*	Felis silvestris			+	+
Pardel Lynx*	Lynx pardellus			+	
Wild Boar*	Sus scrofa			+	
Fallow Deer*	Dama dama			+	
Red Deer*	Cervus elaphus			+	

BIBLIOGRAPHY

ALFONSO XI: *El Libro de la Montería;* Madrid, 1877.
ALVAREZ, F.: *Nidificación de Cyanopica cyana y Pica pica en Doñana;* Doñana-Acta vert. Sevilla, 1974.
ARGOTE DE MOLINA: *Discurso sobre la montería;* Madrid, 1882.
BERNIS, F. y VALVERDE, J. A.: *Sur le flamand rose dans la peninsule Iberique;* Alauda, 1953.
BERNIS, F. y VALVERDE, J. A.: *La gran colonia de garzas del Coto Doñana;* Munibe, 1954.
BERNIS, F. y VALVERDE, J. A.: *Sobre la garza real en España;* Bol. Soc. Esp. Hist. Nat., 1954.
BLAS ARITIO, L.: *Guía de campo de los mamíferos españoles;* SPCPN, Madrid, 1971.
BRUUN Y SINGER: *Guía de las aves de Europa;* Ed. Omega, Barcelona, 1971.
CAMPBELL Y FERGUSON-LEES: *A Field Guide to Birds Nests;* Constable, London, 1972.
CONDE DE YEBES: *Veinte años de caza mayor;* Espasa-Calpe, Madrid, 1943.
CHAPMAN, A.: *Wild Spain;* Jurney and Jackson; London, 1893.
CHAPMAN, A.: *Unexplored Spain;* Arnold, London, 1910.
CHAPMAN, A.: *Memories;* Jurney and Jackson, London, 1930.
CHAPMAN, A.: *Retrospect;* Jurney and Jackson, London, 1928.
CHAPMAN, A.: *Rough notes on Spanish Ornithology;* Ibis, 1884.
CHOCOMELI, J.: *En busca de Tartessos;* Valencia, 1940.
DOMÍNGUEZ, A.: *Notas recopiladas sobre el Coto de Doña Ana.*
DOTRENS, E.: *Batraciens et reptiles d'Europe;* Delachaux et Niestlé, Neuchatel, 1967.
DUCLÓS, C.: *Excursión Ornitológica por el Sur de Andalucía;* Bol. R. Soc. Esp. Hist., 1953.
DUQUE DE ALMAZÁN: *Historia de la montería en España;* Madrid, 1934.
ESQUERRE DEL BAYO, J.: *La duquesa de Alba y Goya;* Editorial Aguilar, Madrid, 1959.
FERNÁNDEZ, J. A.: *Tierras de Doñana;* Archivo Hispalense. Sevilla, 1968.
FERNÁNDEZ, J. A.: *Guía del Parque Nacional de Doñana;* Public. Minist. Agricultura. Madrid, 1974.
GARCÍA MERCADAL, J.: *¿Quién fue la Princesa de Eboli?;* Madrid, 1959.
GRANDE COBIÁN, R.: *Los suelos salinos;* Public. Minist. de Agricultura, Madrid, 1956.
GUINEA, E.: *Flora básica;* Madrid, 1961.
HAINARD, R.: *Les mammiferes sauvages de l'Europe;* Delachaux et Niestlé, Neuchatel, 1948.
INFANTE GALÁN, J.: *Rocio;* Ed. Prensa Española, Sevilla, 1971.
LE MONDE ILLUSTRÉ: Vol. 13, París, 1863.
MARAÑÓN, G.: *Antonio Pérez;* Espasa-Calpe, Madrid, 1960.
MARAÑÓN, G.: *El Conde-Duque de Olivares;* Espasa-Calpe, Madrid, 1952.
MARQUÉS DE ALBENTOS: *Arte general de cacerías y monterías;* Sevilla, 1862.
MARQUÉS DEL SALTILLO: *El Duque de Medina-Sidonia y la jornada de Inglaterra en 1588;* Santander, 1934.
MAURA GAMAZO, G.: *El designio de Felipe II y el episodio de la Armada Invencible;* Ed. Cultura Clásica y Moderna, Madrid, 1957.
MOUNTFORT, G.: *The Herons of the Coto Doñana;* The Sphere, 1956.
MOUNTFORT, G.: *Rare birds in the Coto Doñana;* The Sphere, 1956.
MOUNTFORT, G.: *A rare bird: the Spanish Imperial Eagle;* The Times, 1957.
MOUNTFORT, G.: *First pictures of the Spanish Imperial Eagle;* The Sphere, 1957.
MOUNTFORT, G.: *The Short-Toed Eagle at Home;* The Sphere, 1957.
MOUNTFORT, G.: *Portrait of a Wilderness;* Hutchinson. London, 1958.
MOUNTFORT, G.: *Sanctuary in Andalucía;* Natural History, 1958.
NICHOLSON, FERGUSON-LEES, HOLLON: *The Camargue and the Coto Doñana;* British Birds, 1957.
PAN ELBERTO, C.: *El Coto Doñana;* Rev. Cinegética Ilustrada, 1928.
PETERSON, R. T.: *Rare Birds Flock to Spain's Marismas;* The Natural Geograph. Mag., 1958.
PETERSON, MOUNFORT, HOLLOM: *A Field guide to the Birds of Britain and Europe.* Collins, 1954.
POLUNIN, O. Y SMYTHIES, B. E.: *Flowers of South-West Europe;* Oxford U.P. London, 1973.
PFANDL, L.: *Felipe II;* Ed. Cultura Española. Madrid, 1942.
RUBIO, J. M.: *Tercera expedición de anillamiento en Doñana;* Munibe, 1955.
SÁNCHEZ, R.: *Revista Gaditana;* Cádiz, 1840.
SCHULTEN, A.: *Tartessos;* Espasa-Calpe. Madrid, 1945.
STEWARD, J. W.: *The Snakes of Europe;* David-Charles. Newton Abbot. Devon, 1971.
STEWARD, J. W.: *The Tailed Amphibians of Europe.* Newton Abbot. Devon, 1969.
VAN DEN BRINK: *Guide des mammiferes sauvages de l'Europe occidentale;* Delachaux et Niestlé. Neuchatel, 1967.
VALVERDE, J. A.: *Notes ecologiques sur le lynx de l'Espagne;* La Terre et la Vie, 1957.
VALVERDE, J. A.: *An Ecological Sketch of the Coto Doñana;* British Birds, 1958.
VALVERDE, J. A.: *Vertebrados de las marismas del Guadalquivir;* Arch. Inst. Aclim. de Almería, 1960.
VALVERDE, J. A.: *Estructura de una comunidad de vertebrados terrestres;* C.S.I.C., Madrid, 1967.
VERNER, W.: *My Life Among the wild Birds in Spain;* London, 1909.
WITHERBY, H.: *Two Months in the Guadalquivir;* Knowledge, 1899.

The publishers wish to express their gratitude to Union Explosivos Rio Tinto, S. A. whose generous cooperation due to their interest in the conservation of nature, has facilitated the publication of this work.

THE PHOTOGRAPHS ARE FROM:

CAMOYAN, A.: 23, 60, 66, 88, 92, 128, 157, 192, 227, 231 y 237 — BAUFLE, J. M.: 148 y 159 — DIAZ DE LOS REYES, A.: 15, 98, 134, 166, 209, 220, 222, 223, 226, 230 y 240 — MELGAREJO, C.: 218 y 241 — ONTAÑON, F.: 114, 115, 142 y 149 — ORONOZ: 13, 19, 21, 27 y 28 — PAISAJES ESPAÑOLES: 45 — PECHUAN, L.: 56, 126, 127, 137, 164, 217, 219 y 243 — PONS, J. R.: 64, 74, 103, 106, 112, 121, 144, 153, 162, 189 y 201 — SAAVEDRA, S.: 72, 138, 177 y 237 — SARRO, A.: 54, 63, 91, 96, 104, 118, 122, 129, 136, 168, 186 y 194 — SETOAIN: 150 — SILVA, A.: 101 — SUETENS VAN GROENDAEL: 146, 165 y 184 — TORES, A.: 75 — VAVRA, R.: 198 — YBARRA, A.: 34, 46 y 38 — THE AUTHOR: 17, 24, 31, 32, 43, 46, 48, 50, 52, 59, 62, 65, 69, 70, 76, 77, 81, 82, 84, 87, 94, 105, 107, 108, 110, 117, 124, 125, 131, 132, 133, 139, 141, 151, 155, 160, 168, 169, 178, 180, 183, 190, 203, 204, 205, 208, 210, 212, 214, 222, 225, 228, 229, 232, 233, 235, 236, 238, 239, 242, 244, 245 y 246.

CONTENTS

Map of Migratory Routes	4
Map of Coto Doñana	6
Foreword	9
Introduction	11
The Glorious Past	12
Corrals and Dunes	44
Pines and Lakes	78
Scrubland of Doñana	109
Ancient Cork Oak Trees	142
Sovereigns of Doñana	175
Marshes	202
Epilogue	248
List of the Zoological Species	250
Bibliography	253

Printed By
Imprenta Sevillana S. A.
Paper estucado Printomat
by Sarrió C.P.L.S.A.
Color Reproduction
By Llovet S. A.
Composition Imposa
Binding And Realisation
Imprenta Sevillana S. A.
Dos Hermanas (Sevilla)